HOW TO
DEAL WITH
POXES

(ON A DAILY BASIS)

THIS IS FOR ALL THE POXES I'VE EVER COME ACROSS. YES YOU, FOR WALKING THROUGH THE DOOR WHILE MY MUSCLES SEIZED UP IN MY LEFT ARM AS I STOOD THERE WAITING, SMILING, HOLDING A DOOR THREE TIMES MY WEIGHT AS YOU SLOWLY WALKED OUT WITH YOUR WEEKLY FROM TESCO, NOT A BOTHER ON YE AS I SCREAMED, 'YOU'RE WELCOME!'.

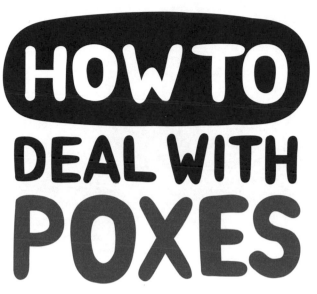

HOW TO
DEAL WITH
POXES
(ON A DAILY BASIS)

WRITTEN AND ILLUSTRATED BY
AOIFE DOOLEY

GILL BOOKS

GILL BOOKS
HUME AVENUE
PARK WEST
DUBLIN 12
WWW.GILLBOOKS.IE

GILL BOOKS IS AN IMPRINT OF M.H. GILL & CO.

© AOIFE DOOLEY 2017

978 0717I 7946 6

PRINTED BY BZ GRAF, POLAND

THE PAPER USED IN THIS BOOK COMES FROM THE WOOD PULP OF MANAGED FORESTS. FOR EVERY TREE FELLED, AT LEAST ONE TREE IS PLANTED, THEREBY RENEWING NATURAL RESOURCES.

A CIP CATALOGUE RECORD FOR THIS BOOK IS AVAILABLE FROM THE BRITISH LIBRARY.

5 4 3 2 1

PRAISE FOR AOIFE'S FIRST BOOK,
HOW TO BE MASSIVE

'FUNNY, AFFECTIONATE, AND VERY, VERY SHARP
... THIS BOOK IS – WELL – MASSIVE.'
RODDY DOYLE

'A VERY FUNNY SLICE OF WORKING-CLASS LIFE.'
THE IRISH TIMES

'WICKEDLY FUNNY.'
THE SUNDAY WORLD

'THIS BOOK HAS ME F**KIN' SCREAMING ...
IF YOU HAVE HUNS IN YOUR LIFE, THIS IS
WHAT YOU NEED TO BUY THEM.'
JAMES KAVANAGH

FROM COOLOCK, AOIFE DOOLEY'S POPULAR ILLUSTRATIONS ABOUT LIFE ON THE NORTHSIDE OF DUBLIN FIRST BECAME A HIT ON INSTAGRAM. HER FIRST BOOK BASED ON THESE ILLUSTRATIONS, HOW TO BE MASSIVE, WAS PUBLISHED IN 2016. HER WORK HAS BEEN SHARED BY SPIN 1038, TODAY FM, JOE.IE, HER.IE AND THE DAILY EDGE. IT HAS ALSO FEATURED IN THE IRISH TIMES, STELLAR MAGAZINE, XPOSÉ, OFFSET AND ON THE IAN DEMPSEY SHOW. SHE HAS RECENTLY BEGUN MAKING REGULAR APPEARANCES AS A STAND-UP COMEDIAN ON THE DUBLIN COMEDY SCENE, INCLUDING THE VODAFONE COMEDY FESTIVAL IN 2017.

CONTENTS

ANATOMY OF A POX

THIS IS ME BESTO TANYA. I LOVE HER TO BITS BUT SHE'S THE DEFINITION OF A POX. WRECKS ME HEAD ON A DAILY BASIS, STOP!

ROBBED ME FAVOURITE JUMPER AN' GOT A CURRY STAIN ON IT

DOESN'T GIVE A RAT'S ARSE

CRUSTY FLUFFY SOCKS

PIZZA SLICE ON ME NEW CARPET

POXES
IN YOUR GAFF

THERE'S ALWAYS ONE POX IN YIZZER GAFF WHO WRECKS YOUR HEAD
CONSTANTLY. FROM PUTTIN' EMPTY BOTTLES OF COKE BACK IN THE
FRIDGE TO NOT CHANGIN' THE TOILET ROLL WHEN IT RUNS OUT - DON'T
EVEN GET ME STARTED. HERE'S A FEW WAYS THA' YE CAN DEAL WITH THEM
SO THEY'LL STOP DOIN' THE THINGS THA' ANNOY YE THE MOST.

5

POXES WHO ROB
YIZZER FOOD

ROB ME FREDDO
BAR AN' YOU'RE
A DEAD MAN

DO YE EVER JUST GET A LOVELY BAR OF CHOCOLATE AND SAY TO YIZZERSELF, 'NOW, GONNA ENJOY THA' LATER WHEN I'M WATCHIN' GEORDIE SHORE WITH A CUPPA TEA', BUT NEXT THING YE KNOW YOU'RE PULLIN' THE FRIDGE APART LOOKIN' FOR A POXY CARAMEL FREDDO BAR ONLY TO FIND THA' SOME LIL' TICK HAS ROBBED IT ON YE? HERE'S WHA' YE DO SO IT DOESN'T HAPPEN AGAIN.

WHA' YE CAN DO

WRAP AN APPLE IN THE TINFOIL
FROM AN EASTER EGG TO GIVE
THE ILLUSION THA' IT'S CHOCOLATE.

FILL UP THE EMPTY BOTTLE OF
COKE YE FOUND IN THE FRIDGE
WITH PRUNE JUICE.

STICK PICTURES OF THE FOOD THA'
WAS ROBBED ON YE AROUND THE
HOUSE AN' LABLE IT 'MISSING'.

HIDE THE GOOD STUFF WHERE
POXES DON'T BOTHER LOOKIN' ...
LIKE THE WASHIN' MACHINE.

POXES WHO PUT
WRAPPERS DOWN THE SIDES
OF THE CHAIR

LIKE A KINDER
SURPRISE
EXCEPT THE
SURPRISE IS
ROTTEN!

DOWN THE SIDES OF THE CHAIRS IN MY GAFF ARE LIKE NARNIA - YE
NEVER KNOW WHA' YOU'LL POXY FIND. I FOUND 50 EURDO ONCE AN' I
WAS JUST LIKE, 'SOUND! SPICEBAG SORTED FOR LATER AN' A FEW BITS
AN' PIECES IN PENNEYS, LOVELY'. I DON'T MIND FINDIN' MONEY BUT I
HATE WHEN I FIND WRAPPERS OFF OF BARS AN' CRIPS DOWN THERE.

THINGS YE FIND DOWN THE SIDES OF A CHAIR

YOUR GRANDA'S TEETH

RICH TEA AN' COOKIE CRUMBS

THE REMOTE CONTROL

WEDDIN' RING LOST FOR FIVE YEARS

A TENNER! YEOOWW!

AN' IPHONE ON SILENT THAT'S BEEN MISSIN' FOR WEEKS

POXES WHO SAY
'YEAH, I WILL IN A MINUTE'

THIS IS DERMO 'YEAH, I WILL IN A MINUTE' O'REILLY, MY ANTO'S MATE.
HE'S ALWAYS SAYIN' TO HIS BIRD LAUREN, 'YEAH, I WILL IN A MINUTE',
AN' THE POX TAKES ABOUT TWO BLEEDIN' HOURS TO GET UP TO HELP
HER DO SOMETHIN'. WRECKS ME HEAD. I TAUGHT HER A FEW TRICKS
AN' NOW THE POX IS ALWAYS UP FASTER THAN' A BOLT OF LIGHTNIN'.

WHA' TO SAY

HERE'S A FEW THINGS YE CAN SAY TO A LAZY POX THA' WILL GET THEM UP OUT OF THEIR CHAIR IN 2.5 SECONDS. AS I SAID, I TAUGHT LAUREN A FEW OF ME TRICKS AN' THEY ALWAYS WORK. ESPECIALLY THE FAIR CITY ONE. IF YE HAVE KIDS THA' DO FUCK ALL IN THE GAFF, JUST TELL THEM THA' THE CHAIR THEY'RE SITTIN' IN WAS THE ONE THA' THEY WERE CONCEIVED IN AN' I TELL YE SOMETHIN', THEY'LL MOVE THA' FAST THA' YE COULD PUT A HORSE MASK ON THEM AND ENTER THEM INTO THE RACES.

POXES WHO DON'T
CHANGE THE TOILET ROLL

WILL EVERYONE PLEASE JUST STOP POXY DOIN' THIS? SOUND.

THERE'S ONLY ONE THING WORSE THAN GOIN' FOR A NO.2 AN' REALISING THA' THERE'S NO TOILET ROLL IN THE JAX, AN' THAT'S POXES WHO TAKE THE LAST LIL' BIT OF THE ROLL AN' LEAVE THE EMPTY CARDBOARD BIT THERE. EH, SORRY, NOT BEIN' FUNNY BUT BLEEDIN' CHANGE THE THING?! TAKES, LIKE, TWO SECONDS.

HOW TO GET THEM BACK

FAKE SPIDER

PUT A FAKE SPIDER IN THE TOILET ROLL TO GIVE THEM A HEART ATTACK.

FAKE USED JOHNNY

PVA glue

XXL

STICK A GREASY JOHNNY ON THE ROLL SO WHEN THEY CHANGE IT THEY'LL TOUCH IT.

FAKE SHIT

LOOKS LIKE REAL SHIT

WHEN MIXED WITH WATER, THE CARDBOARD ROLL LOOKS LIKE A LUMP OF SHITE.

PURE BLACKMAIL

I KNOW UR PASSWORD

WRITE MESSAGES ON THE TOILET ROLL TO BLACKMAIL THEM INTO CHANGIN' IT THE NEXT TIME.

13

POXES WHO LEAVE
RUNNERS ON THE STAIRS

AH YEAH, I'LL JUST LEAVE THESE
WHERE SOMEONE CAN POTENTIALLY
FALL OVER AN' BREAK THEIR NECK.

YE EVER COME IN FROM A NIGH' OUT CREEPIN' AROUND THE GAFF
TRYIN' NOT TO WAKE ANYONE UP, AN' YOU'VE ALMOST MADE IT TO
YIZZER ROOM WITHOUT A SOUND UNTIL YE TRIP OVER SOME TICK'S
RUNNERS THA' THEY LEFT ON THE STAIRS? GREAT PLACE TO LEAVE
THEM. SOUND. WELL, YE WON'T BE LEAVIN' THEM THERE AGAIN AFTER
I'M DONE WITH YE.

WHEN YE CAN'T COPE

ANY OF THESE FOUR THINGS WILL WORK AN' THE POX
WILL GET THE PICTURE. THEY'LL BE PURE SNAPPIN'.

PUT THEM UP FOR SALE
IN YIZZER FRONT GARDEN.

PUT ONE OF THEM FAKE
TOILET ROLL SHITES IN
THE RUNNER.

PIN THEM OVER THEIR BEDROOM
DOOR SO WHEN THEY WALK OUT
THEY'LL HIT THEM IN THE HEAD.

PUT A FISH OR ANYTHIN'
THA' SMELLS PURE ROTTEN
IN THE RUNNER.

POXES WITH MOULDY MUGS

WE ALL HAVE OUR FAVOURITE MUGS IN OUR GAFFS, MUGS THA' IF ANYONE WRAPPED THEIR LIPS AROUND YOU'D GIVE THEM A SLAP. TANYA IS ALWAYS ROBBIN' ME MUGS AN' LEAVIN' THEM TO GO MOULDY IN HER ROOM, AN' IT'S BLEEDIN' ROTTEN. DO BE GOIN' INTO HER ROOM WITH A MASK ON SO I DON'T GET RIDDLED WITH SOME KIND OF GONE-OFF TEA DISEASE. YE CAN NEVER BE TOO CAREFUL THESE DAYS, SWEAR.

WHA' YE CAN DO

IF IT GETS MOULDY TO THE MAX
THEN TAKE A PIC AN' TAG THE
ROTTEN POX ON FACEBOOK.

LEAVE A LIL' NOTE SO THE
POX KNOWS NOT TO GO NEAR
YIZZER FAVOURITE MUG.

ALWAYS LEAVE A LIPSTICK STAIN
ON YIZZER MUG SO NO ONE
TAKES IT ON YE.

GIVE THEM THE 'IF YE TOUCH ME
MUG AGAIN I'LL STREEL OUT OF YE'
LOOK AN' THEY'LL GET THE PICTURE.

POXES WHO DON'T WASH UP

AH YEAH, JUST LEAVE YIZZER DIRTY DISHES THERE AN' LEAVE THE
GAFF. SEE YE LATER, DAY-DAY. SWEAR, HATE WHEN POXES LEAVE
DIRTY DISHES LYIN' AROUND THE GAFF. ANTO'S ALWAYS DOIN' IT AND
HE EATS LIKE A BLEEDIN' HORSE. DON'T KNOW HOW HE DOES IT - POX
IS STILL SKINNIER THAN I AM AN' I'M ON SLIMMIN' WORLD.

DISH DIAGRAM

COCO POP BOWL
FROM YESTERDAY

ME DA'S
CODDLE

DON'T KNOW WHA'
WAS IN THA' BOWL
BUT LOOKS LIKE A
POXY CRIME SCENE

CURRY FROM
THE WEEKEND

EH, WASH THE KETCHUP OFF,
DON'T JUST LEAVE IT THERE
- SWEAR, PACK OF ANIMALS

CHIPPER FROM FRIDAY

POXES
IN YOUR JOB

WHEN YOU'RE IN WORK THE LAST THING YE WANT IS TO BE SURROUNDED BY SAPS FOR HOURS ON END. FROM POXES WHO GO TO THE GYM AN' BRAG ABOUT IT TO YOUR BOSS BEIN' A BALLBAG FOR NO REASON. THIS CHAPTER WILL GIVE YE TIPS ON HOW TO COPE.

ME IN WORK

MOST OF THE TIME WHEN I'M IN WORK I'M DOIN' FUCK ALL AN' JUST HAVIN' A LAUGH WITH THE GIRLS. LAST THING I WANT TO DO WHEN I'M HUNGOVER IS WORK FOR SOME POX WHO'S BEIN' A SAP FOR NO REASON AN' WRECKIN' ME WHOLE DAY.

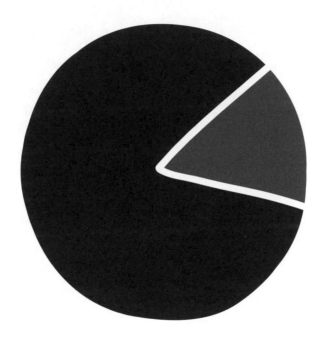

AMOUNT OF TIME I SPEND DOIN' NOTHIN'

AMOUNT OF TIME I SPEND DOIN' ACTUAL WORK

HOW TO LOOK LIKE YOU'RE DOIN' WORK WHEN YOU'RE DOIN' FUCK ALL

TO GIVE YOUR BOSS THE ILLUSION THA' YOU'RE A HARD WORKER, STARE BLANKLY AT A PAGE TO SHOW THA' YOU'RE TRYIN' TO WORK SOMETHIN' OUT, BUT WHA' YOU'RE REALLY DOIN' IS LOOKIN' AT A PICK-ME-UP MAGAZINE AND READIN' AN ARTICLE ABOUT SOME YOUNG FELLA WHO DITCHED HIS BIRD TO MARRY A GOAT IN MAYO. LOOKIN' DEEP IN THOUGHT WORKS WONDERS AS WELL.

POXES WHO ALWAYS TALK ABOUT THE GYM

'THE GUNS'

'THE SWANS'

FLASHIN' A BIT OF THE KNEE TAN, COS MOTHS ARE ONLY MAD FOR TANNED KNEES

BAG FULL OF TANNERS

'WHAT'S A LEG DAY?' LEGS

YOU'RE A SAP IF YE ...

... DO ANY OF THE THINGS BELOW. YE WANT A SIX PACK? THEN WORK FOR IT. YE WANT A NICE TAN? THEN DO A POXY SUN BED. DON'T BE BUYIN' TANNIN' INJECTIONS OFF SOME BLOKE IN THE GYM CARPARK. SWEAR! THESE KINDS OF FELLAS THINK THEY'RE GOD'S BLEEDIN' GIFT BUT THEY LOOK ROTTEN.

- USE TANNERS

- TAKE STEROIDS

- POST PICS OF YIZZER SIX PACK DAILY

- THINK YOU'RE THE IMAGE OF TOM HARDY

POXES WHO GO ON DIETS EVERY SECOND WEEK

THE ONES YE WRAP AROUND YIZZER BELLY, NOT THE ONES YE EAT

SKINNY GEE tea

SLIMMIN' wraps

SWEAR, IF I SEE ONE MORE POX TRYIN' TO ADD ME TO A SKINNY TEA GROUP ON FACEBOOK I'LL SNAP. DON'T BE TRYIN' TO SELL ME YIZZER BANJAXED GEE TEA COS I'VE SEEN THE EFFECTS. A FEW OF THE GIRLS IN WORK HAVE TRIED IT AN' THE MOOD SWINGS ON THEM! POOR AUL DEARBHLA ON THE TILLS HASN'T HAD ANY SUGAR IN THREE DAYS AN' SHE'S LOST HER BLEEDIN' MIND, SOBBIN' EVERY TWO SECONDS.

WHA' YE CAN DO

EAT ME

IF YE SEE SOMEONE IN DISTRESS FROM NOT EATIN' ANY SUGAR, GET THEM SOMETHIN' FULL OF THE SHIT. I BOUGHT AUL DEARBHLA A FEW DOUGHNUTS EARLIER ON AN' YE SWEAR I WAS AFTER BUYIN' HER A WINNIN' LOTTO TICKET OR SOMETHIN'. IF YOU'RE TRYIN' TO LOSE WEIGH' THEN DO IT THE HEALTHY WAY, COS NONE OF THESE FAD DIETS WORK AN' YE JUST END UP DEPRIVIN' YIZZERSELF.

POXES WHO NAME DROP

GEORGE CLOONEY SIDE BOOBED ME IN TESCO

I THINK IT WAS GEORGE CLOONEY

THERE'S ALWAYS ONE POX IN THE JOB WHO NAME DROPS. 'AH YEAH, I KNOW KEITH DUFFY VERY WELL. I MET HIM ONCE IN THE OMNI. SWEAR, IT WRECKS ME HEAD. YE KNOW IT DOESN'T MAKE YIZZER LIFE MORE INTERESTIN' BY NAME DROPPIN' POXES THA' YOU'VE ONLY MET ONCE IN THE SHOPS. HERE'S HOW I DEAL WITH PEOPLE WHO ARE ALWAYS NAME DROPPIN'.

NAME DROP BACK

WHEN SOME POX ROBS YIZZER LUNCH

YE EVER BRING IN A LOVELY BIT OF BIRTHDAY CAKE OR SOMETHIN'
FOR YIZZER LUNCH AN' THEN SOME SICK ANIMAL IN WORK EATS IT
ON YE? YEAH, HAPPENS TO ME ALL THE TIME, SO NOW I DISGUISE
IT AS SOMETHIN' ROTTEN SO THEY DON'T BOTHER LOOKIN' IN THE
LUNCH BOX OR TINFOIL. BLEEDIN' VULTURES IN MY WORK. THEY'D
EAT A CORN FLAKE OFF A DUCK'S MICKEY.

HOW TO HIDE CAKE FROM VULTURES

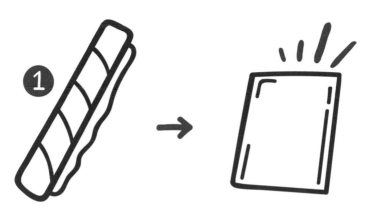

1 CUT OUT A NICE LIL' SQUARE OF THE AUL TINFOIL SO YE CAN USE IT TO HIDE YIZZER CAKE.

2 MASSIVE BISCUIT CAKE

PAUL'S ROTTEN SANDWICH

3 WRAP IT UP AN' PUT A STICKER ON IT SAYIN' IT'S SOMETHIN' ROTTEN.

POXES WHO CONSTANTLY TALK ABOUT THEIR KIDDIES

'AH, LOOK AT ME SON. HE COULD WALK WHEN HE WAS TWO WEEKS OLD.' AWH, WOULD YE GIVE IT POXY OVER. NOTHIN' WORSE THAN WHEN SOMEONE TALKS ABOUT THEIR KIDS CONSTANTLY AN' YOU'RE JUST THERE LIKE, 'YEAH, I ACTUALLY HAVE TO GO, ME BUS IS DUE IN FIVE MINUTES, HUN'. HERE'S HOW YE GET SOMEONE TO STOP TALKIN' TO YE ABOUT THEIR KIDS.

SHOW THEM YOUR KIDDIE

ME BRICK

15.10.17

'AH, ME LIL' BRICK. HE'S GROWIN' UP SO FAST. NEXT THING I KNOW HE'LL BE TOWERIN' OVER ME.'

SHOW THEM A PICTURE OF A RANDOM OBJECT OF YIZZER CHOICE. IT CAN BE ANYTHIN' YE WANT, BUT THE WEIRDER THE BETTER. I LIKE TO KEEP THIS PICTURE OF A BRICK, AN' I HAVE ONE ON ME PHONE TOO. WHEN YE SHOW THEM THEY'LL EITHER THINK YOU'RE A WEIRDO OR THEY'LL GET THE HINT THA' THEY TALK ABOUT THEIR KIDS WAY TOO MUCH.

POXES WHO BITCH BEHIND YIZZER BACK

THERE'S ALWAYS ONE PERSON IN YIZZER WORK WHO'S ALL NICE TO YIZZER FACE AN' THEN BITCHES BEHIND YIZZER BACK. DON'T WORRY, HUN, I CAN SEE RIGH' THROUGH YE JUST LIKE I CAN SEE RIGH' THROUGH YIZZER WORN-OUT LEGGINS. WELL, KARMA'S A BITCH AN' YE NEVER BITCH TO A HUN'S GOOD FRIEND COS IT ALWAYS COMES BACK AROUND, YE TICK. HERE'S WHA' I DO TO ME HATERS.

GIVE THEM THE EYES

THESE ARE ME SIGNATURE LOOKS THA' YOUS CAN USE
WHEN SOMEONE IS BEIN' A SAP AN' TALKIN' ABOUT YE.

LOOK THEM DOWN

NOW LOOK THEM UP

LOOK AWAY AN' SMILE

THE 'OH, SHE'S
WEARIN' KITTEN HEELS'

THE 'I KNOW WHA'
YE SAID ABOUT ME'

THE 'ARE YOU FOR
POXY REAL, LUV?'

WHEN YOUR BOSS IS A BALLBAG

YOU ATE ALL OF THE DOUGHNUTS FROM THE BAKERY

IN TWO HOURS

SEAN

ME FRIEND TANYA'S BOSS IS ALWAYS GOIN' ON A MAD ONE AT HER. SHE GOT IN TROUBLE FOR EATIN' ALL THE DOUGHNUTS FROM THE BAKERY ONCE. I HATE IT WHEN YE GET CALLED INTO THE OFFICE FOR SOMETHIN'. YE DO BE BRICKIN' IT AN' THEN IT DOES BE OVER SOMETHIN' STUPID LIKE YIZZER TILL WAS DOWN A CENT. SOME BOSSES GO ON A PURE POWER TRIP AN' IT WRECKS ME HEAD.

EXCUSES FOR CALLIN' IN SICK
(WHEN YOU'RE HUNGOVER)

WHEN YE GO OUT FOR JUST ONE DRINK WITH THE GIRLS AN' IT
ENDS UP BEIN', LIKE, SIX AN' TWO JAGER BOMBS, YOU'LL NEED A FEW
EXCUSES TO GET OUT OF GOIN' INTO WORK THE NEXT DAY WHEN
YE CAN'T DEAL WITH THE PURE STRESS. NO ONE'S GONNA QUESTION
YE IF YOU'VE LEFT A CHICKEN IN THE OVEN.

WAS ON THE
BUS WHEN I
REMEMBERED
THA' I LEFT
A CHICKEN IN
THE OVEN

ME HEAD IS
HURTIN' ME
FACE AN' ALL

I THINK
I'M COMIN'
DOWN WITH THE
PRINGLES

JOB STICKERS

IMAGIN' YE HAD A RANGE OF STICKERS FOR ALL THE DIFFERENT TYPES OF POXES IN YIZZER JOB. THA' BE GAS.

WHAT'S YOUR WORK NICKNAME?

MONTH YE WERE BORN

FIRST LETTER OF YIZZER NAME

JAN LIL'

FEB MOANY

MAR GOOPY

APR MASSIVE

MAY ANGRY

JUN WET

JUL DAMP

AUG DROOPY

SEP STICKY

OCT PIGEON

NOV ROTTEN

DEC SMELLY

A FRUIT FLAPS

B COTTON SOCKS

C CAMEL TOE

D CALCULATOR TICK

E COFFEE WANKER

F GYM GREMLIN

G PRINGLE FLAPS

H GIN AN' TONIC SAP

I BOSS BITCH

J SAUSAGE ROLL BREATH

K SUIT POX

L HOOP LICKER

M SALAD TICK

N QUIVERIN' NIPPLES

O COTTON SOCKS

P ARM FLEX TICK

Q LONG FACED DOPE

R FANNY WIG

S LICKY LICK ARSE

T SALSA BALLS

U SAUSAGE ROLL SAP

V MICKEY RIDDLER

W MONDAY SAP

X BOSS HOOP

Y CREAM CRACKER TICK

Z FRIDGET BREATH

POXES
ON PUBLIC
TRANSPORT

AH, PUBLIC TRANSPORT, WHERE PEOPLE BRING ON ROTTEN SMELLIN' FOOD AN' DON'T GIVE UP THEIR SEATS FOR OLD LADIES. THE WORST KIND OF POXES ARE THE POXES YOU MEET ON PUBLIC TRANSPORT. THIS CHAPTER GOES THROUGH EVERYTHIN' FROM POXES WHO HOG SEATS TO TYPES OF BUS DRIVERS AN' HOW TO GET THROUGH A JOURNEY WHEN YOU'RE SURROUNDED BY SAPS.

KIDS TODAY WILL NEVER KNOW THE PURE JOY OF LOOKIN' DOWN THE WINDOW ON THE BUS AND SEEIN' THE BUS DRIVER'S BALDY HEAD

TYPES OF BUS DRIVERS

MOST BUS DRIVERS YE MEET ARE SOUND, LET'S BE HONEST. BUT THERE'S ALWAYS ONE OR TWO THA' YE COME ACROSS WHO ARE HORRIBLE POXES THE WAY THEY TALK TO YE. LIKE, THERE'S NO NEED FOR IT, PAL. ALRIGH', IF YOU'RE HAVIN' A BAD DAY OR YE SPILLED YIZZER BOWL OF COCO POPS THIS MORNIN', FAIR ENOUGH, BUT YE DON'T NEED TO TAKE IT OUT ON ME.

THE ONE WHO KEEPS DRIVIN' WHEN HE SEES YE RUNNIN'

THE ONE WHO LETS YE ON WHEN YOU'RE SHORT A FEW BOB

THE ONE WHO'S 20 MINUTES LATE

THE ONE WHO LETS YE ON WHEN IT'S RAININ' EVEN IF HE'S NOT LEAVIN' FOR FIVE MINUTES

THE ONE WHO TELLS YE YOUR STOP IS COMIN' UP WHEN YOU'RE NOT SURE

THE ONE WHO'S BEEN ON THE SAME ROUTE SINCE YE WERE A KID

POXES WHO BRING FOOD ON THE BUS

YE SEE WHEN YOU'RE COMIN' HOME FROM TOWN AN' SOME GEEBAG GETS ON THE BUS WITH HOT FOOD? STOP! YOU'RE IN A CONFINED SPACE WITH LIKE 60 OR 70 OTHER PEOPLE, PAL. HAVE SOME BLEEDIN' DECENCY! NOT EVERYONE WANTS TO SMELL YIZZER ROTTEN FOOD AFTER A HARD DAY IN WORK, ESPECIALLY WHEN IT'S A POXY KEBAB.

TOP FOOD ON THE BUS

STALE MCDONALD'S

A BIG DIRTY PIZZA SLICE

JAMBONS 0.75c

JAMBONS FIRST THING IN THE POXY MORNIN'

SPAR SAUSAGE ROLLS - THE FLAKES DO BE ALL OVER THE GAFF

A TUNA ROLL - GOD SAVE US BLEEDIN' ALL

PHONE POXES

JUST ON THE BUS

HEAD TILTED SO IF YOU'RE SITTIN' BEHIND THEM YE CAN'T SEE YIZZER STOP COMIN'.

KEEPS TOUCHIN' YE WITH THEIR ELBOW IF YOU'RE SITTIN' BESIDE THEM

SOMETIMES WHEN YE GET THE EARLY BUS HOME YE HAVE THE PURE LUXURY OF NOT HAVIN' TO LISTEN TO SOME DOPE ON THE PHONE TALKIN' FOR THE WHOLE JOURNEY. BUT IF YE DO HAVE TO LISTEN TO ONE, THE BEST THING YE CAN DO IS GIVE THEM THE EYES. LIKE, I DON'T WANT TO BE HEARIN' ABOUT YIZZER WEEKEND AWAY IN GALWAY WITH YIZZER FELLA. COULDN'T GIVE A BOLLOX, ALONG WITH EVERYONE ELSE ON THE BUS. WHY DO THEY TALK SO LOUD?

THINGS POXES LEAVE ON THE BUS

CAN'T FIND ME MA

SOMETIMES SOMEONE LEAVES SOMETHIN' BEHIND AN' IT'S NOT LIKE THEY'RE GONNA COME BACK FOR IT. FOR EXAMPLE, A ROAST CHICKEN. LIKE, AS SOON AS THEY GET OFF THE BUS THEY'RE JUST LIKE, 'AH, ME CHICKEN'. THEY'RE NOT GONNA CALL UP DUBLIN BUS AN' REPORT A MISSIN' CHICKEN SO YE MIGH' AS WELL GIVE IT A NEW HOME. NOW, IF IT'S A WALLET OR SOMETHIN' THEN THAT'S A DIFFERENT STORY. DON'T BE A POX – HAND IT IN TO THE DRIVER.

YOUNG WANS ON THE BUS

KEEPS LOOKIN'
AT YE TO SEE IF
YOU'RE LOOKIN'
AT THEM

JUST SCREAMS
THE WHOLE WAY
BLEEDIN' HOME

NICE FREDDO BAR
BEFORE DINNER

SCHOOL JACKET
THAT'S THREE
TIMES THE SIZE
OF THEM

PHONE IN POCKET
READY TO START
PLAYIN' KYGO

SOCKS THA' LOOK
LIKE THE LAST TIME
THEY WERE WASHED
WAS IN THE LAST
CENTURY

TYPES OF YOUNG WANS

THERE'S FOUR TYPES OF YOUNG WANS YE DO SEE ON THE BUS COMIN' HOME. THEY COME IN SWARMS AN' YE CAN HEAR THEM BEFORE YE POXY SEE THEM! I'VE BROKE IT DOWN FOR YE SO YE KNOW WHA' YOU'RE DEALIN' WITH IF YOU'RE EVER UNFORTUNATE ENOUGH TO BE ON A BUS WITH A LOAD OF FIRST YEARS.

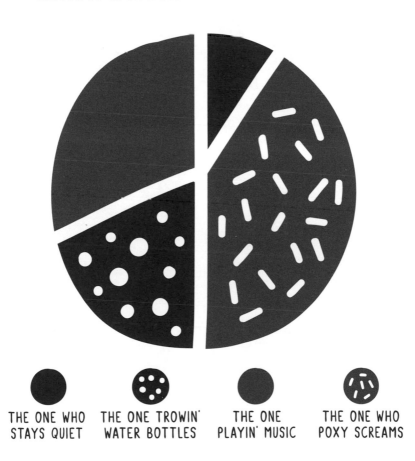

THE ONE WHO STAYS QUIET

THE ONE TROWIN' WATER BOTTLES

THE ONE PLAYIN' MUSIC

THE ONE WHO POXY SCREAMS

POXES WHO COUGH ON YE

HAVE YE EVER JUST HOPPED ON A BUS, MINDIN' YIZZER OWN BUSINESS, LOOKIN' OUT THE WINDOW AT THE HOUSES AN' THINK, 'YE KNOW WHA'? DUBLIN ISN'T ALL A KIP', BUT THEN SOME MANKY ANIMAL SNEEZES OR COUGHS ON YE WITHOUT ANY WARNIN' AN' THEY DON'T EVEN SAY SORRY? IF I DONE THA' I'D BE SCARLEH, BUT NO, NOT THESE POXES. THEY COULDN'T GIVE A RAT'S. IF YE DO THIS YE SHOULD BE ASHAMED OF YIZZERSELF. ASHAMED!

TYPES OF BUS GERMS

THESE ARE THE TYPES OF GERMS THA' HAVE BEEN FOUND ON
PUBLIC TRANSPORT ALL OVER THE CITY. I READ IT IN 'THE SUN'
SO THAT'S HOW I KNOW IT'S 100 PERCENT REAL, SO BE CAREFUL
YE DON'T CATCH ANY OF THESE DEADLY DISEASES THA' ARE GOIN'
AROUND AT THE MOMENT. PLACE IS POXY RIDDLED WITH THEM.

BURNY HOLE
GERM

BLISTERED MICKEY
GERM

ANNOYIN' POX
GERM

STINGY NIPPLE
GERM

DOG BREATH
GERM

SMUG BASTARD
GERM

SEAT HOGGIN' POXES

JUST GONNA LOOK OVER HERE OUT THE WINDOW AN' PRETEND I'VE NO IDEA THE BUS HAS STOPPED AN' THA' MORE PEOPLE ARE GETTIN' ON

GRUNT

AH, THE SEAT HOGGERS. THE POXES ON THE BUS WHO SIT ON THE EDGE OR PUT THEIR BAGS BESIDE THEM SO YE CAN'T SIT DOWN, EVEN THOUGH IT'S POXY RUSH HOUR AN' THERE'S NOWHERE ELSE TO SIT. GRAND, LUV, YOU JUST SIT THERE WITH YIZZER 15 PENNEYS BAGS AN' I'LL JUST GO BACK DOWNSTAIRS AN' STAND THERE LIKE A TICK. SOUND.

HOW TO SPOT THEM

THEY LOOK AWAY WHEN EVERYONE IS GETTIN' ON THE BUS. THEY CAN'T EVEN LOOK YE IN THE EYE.

THEY TAKE UP A WHOLE CHAIR WITH THEIR BAG SO YE CAN'T SIT DOWN.

THEY PRETEND TO BE BUSY TEXTIN' ON THEIR PHONE, BUT WE ALL KNOW WHA' YOU'RE DOIN', PAL.

SOMETIMES THEY TAKE UP THE WHOLE CHAIR AN' SIT IN THE MIDDLE WITH THEIR POXY LEGS SPREAD.

POXES WHO LOOK AT YIZZER PHONE ON THE BUS

DO YE EVER GET THE FEELIN' THA' SOMEONE'S WATCHIN' YE? LIKE SOMEONE'S LOOKIN' AT YE BUT YOU'RE AFRAID TO LOOK COS YE CAN SEE THEM OUT OF THE CORNER OF YIZZER EYE, BUT THEN YE DECIDE TO TAKE A SNEAKY PEAK AN' THEY'RE EYEBALL DEEP IN YIZZER WHATSAPP GROUP MESSAGES. ME FRIEND TANYA IS ALWAYS DOIN' IT TO ME, BUT IT'S EVEN MORE WEIRD WHEN IT'S SOMEONE YE DON'T EVEN KNOW! IMAGINE EYEBALLIN' SOMEONE'S PHONE OUT OF IT AN' YE DON'T EVEN POXY KNOW THEM.

WHA' TO DO

TURN YOUR PHONE TOWARDS THEM SO THEY CAN SEE IT AN' PUT SOMETHIN' ESPECIALLY FOR THEM ON THE SCREEN AN' THEY'LL GET THE PICTURE TO MIND THEIR OWN BLEEDIN' BUSINESS.

A NICE MICKEY ALWAYS GETS THE EYE TO TURN THE OTHER WAY. UNLESS THE PERSON LIKES A LONG MICKEY, IN WHICH CASE YOU'RE FUCKED.

OR YE COULD JUST STRAIGH' UP CALL THEM OUT ON IT.

PUBLIC TRANSPORT SURVIVAL KIT

ANTISEPTIC WASH
FOR POX GERMS

EARPHONES TO BLOCK OUT THE
SOUNDS OF POXES ON THE BUS

EAR PLUGS IF YIZZER
EARS START TO BLEED

CLOTHES PEG FOR YIZZER
NOSE WHEN SOME POX GETS
ON WITH A TUNA ROLL

WHEN YE HAVE NO EARPHONES

WELCOME TO HELL

WHEN YE HAVE NO EARPHONES AN' EVERYONE IS MAKIN' NOISE ON THE BUS, THERE'S FUCK ALL ELSE YE CAN DO OTHER THAN SIT THERE UNTIL YOUR STOP COMES AN' HOPE THA' YOUR EARS DON'T START BLEEDIN' FROM THE SOUNDS OF TEENAGERS SCREAMIN', POSH POXES TALKIN' ABOUT AVOCADOS, BABIES CRYIN' AN' SOMEONE RUSTLIN' THROUGH A BAG OF JOHNNY ONION RINGS AT SEVEN IN THE MORNIN'.

THE UNSPOKEN RULES OF PUBLIC TRANSPORT

THERE YE HAVE IT. THE THINGS YE HAVE TO PUT UP WITH ON PUBLIC TRANSPORT. I HOPE YE LEARNED SOMETHIN' AN YOU'LL REMEMBER THESE VERY IMPORTANT RULES THA' HALF OF YIZ DON'T FOLLOW ANYWAY. SOUND.

DON'T EAT ROTTEN FOOD ON THE BUS

DON'T TALK LOUD ON YIZZER PHONE

DON'T FART ON THE POXY BUS

DON'T HOG THE SEAT LIKE A SPA

COVER YIZZER MOUTH WHEN YE COUGH

BASICALLY, DON'T BE A TICK

WHA' KIND OF PASSENGER ARE YE?

MONTH YE WERE BORN

FIRST LETTER OF YIZZER NAME

JAN ANNOYIN'

FEB WEIRD

MAR CRYIN'

APR SCREAMIN'

MAY ROTTEN

JUN FREAKY

JUL CREEPY

AUG LOUD

SEP CRAZY

OCT OLD

NOV DREARY

DEC SCAULDY

A SEAT HOGGER

B WILLY TOUCHER

C WINDOW LICKER

D TORMENTIN' TICK

E CORN FLAKE POX

F NIPPLE TWIRLER

G HOOP FARTER

H DIDDIE RIDER

I MICKEY MEASURER

J PONY TAIL CUTTER

K CRUSTY HAND FEELER

L CROC WEARIN' POX

M SCHOOL YOUNG WAN

N COFFEE SPITTER

O FLAP SLAPPER

P HOOP HOGGER

Q TOE FEELER

R FLAP TIDDLER

S HAM ROLL SNEEZER

T FLAP RATTLER

U HAIR RUBBER

V EAR LICKIN' POX

W TOE NAIL CLIPPER

X CHIP BAG LEAVER

Y FISH LOVER

Z PHANTOM COUGHER

POXES
ON A DAILY
BASIS

YE MEET SO MANY PEOPLE DAY TO DAY, SO IN THIS CHAPTER YOU'LL SEE THE TYPES OF POXES YE MEET ON A DAILY BASIS. FROM SALES FELLAS TRYIN' TO SELL YE STUFF AT THE DOOR WHEN YOUR MA ISN'T IN TO HIPSTERS AN' POXES WHO GO TO TRINITY.

PREACHERS

JESUS LOVES YOU

WHEN YOU'RE STRUTTIN' AROUND TOWN SHOPPIN' IN A WORLD OF
YOUR OWN, YE ALWAYS HEAR SOMEONE TALKIN' THROUGH ONE OF
THEM BIG SPEAKER YOKES SAYIN' THINGS ABOUT THA' JESUS YOUNG
FELLA AN' THE BIBLE, AN' TRYIN' TO GIVE YE ROSARY BEADS. NOT
BEIN' FUNNY OR ANYTHIN' BUT YOU'RE ALRIGH', LUV. LAST TIME I
WAS IN MASS WAS FOR ME HOLY COMMUNION AN' I CONFESSED TO
ROBBIN' A STINGER BAR FROM THE SHOP.

POXES WHO LIE TO YIZZER ACTUAL FACE

YE EVER GET SOMETHIN' IN YIZZER TEETH, LIKE A BIT OF CHICKEN NUGGET, AN' YE ASK YIZZER SO-CALLED FRIEND, 'IS THERE ANYTHIN' IN ME TEETH OR AM I ALRIGH?', AN' THE POX ALWAYS SAYS, 'YEAH, YOU'RE GRAND HUN'? SAME GOES FOR MAKE-UP WHEN YE HAVE EYELINER ALL OVER THE GAFF AN' NO ONE BOTHERS TO POXY TELL YE. A TRUE FRIEND WOULD TELL SOMEONE WHEN THEY LOOK ROTTEN, JUST SO YIZ KNOW.

WHEN A SEAGULL SHITS ON YE

I'LL SHIT ON YOUR MA

SEE SEAGULLS? THEY'RE THE ACTUAL DEVIL! ALWAYS ROBBIN' ICE CREAMS OFF THE KIDDIES, AN' AS IF THA' ISN'T BAD ENOUGH THE BASTERDIN' THINGS SHIT ON YE AS WELL. WHEN I WAS WALKIN' UP THOMAS STREET BEFORE, ONE OF THEM TOOK A DUMP IN ME RIGH' EYE. THOUGHT I'D BEEN SHOT. I WAS PURE SOBBIN' AT THE BANKLINK UNTIL A WOMAN GAVE ME A TISSUE AN' SAID, 'YOU'RE GRAND, IT'S JUST BIRD SHIT'.

BUY A LOTTO TICKET
OR A SCRATCH CARD

THEY SAY IF A BIRD TAKES A SHIT ON YE THA' IT'S GOOD LUCK SO
BUY A LOTTO TICKET. SWEAR DOWN ON ME LIL' DOG TIESTO'S LIFE
THA' IT IS. ME GRANDA BOUGH' A LOTTO TICKET WHEN IT HAPPENED
TO HIM AN' HE WON SEVEN GRAND. HE WAS CHUFFED WITH HIMSELF.
SO YE KNOW WHA' TO DO NOW THE NEXT TIME IT HAPPENS TO YE.
IMAGINE IF YE WON THE ACTUAL EURDO MILLIONS. STOP!

SLOW WALKIN' POXES

'ARE YE FOR REAL? WE'RE AFTER WALKIN' FOR AGES' FACE

FOR SLAPPIN' POXES WITH WHEN THEY'RE WRECKIN' YIZZER HEAD

HANDBAG FROM RIVER ISLAND THAT'S FULL OF RECEIPTS AN' LIGHTERS

CHICKEN FILLET FROM THE CENTRA IN COULTRY, BALLYMUN. THEY'RE THE BEST!

WHEN YE REALISE IT'S 25 DEGREES OUT AN' YOU'RE PURE SWEATIN' AN' ASK YIZZERSELF, 'WHY DID I WEAR POXY LEGGINS?'

WEARING BRAND NEW AIR MAX OUT ON A WALK AN' GETTING THE FEET CUT OFF YE

FAST WALKIN' POXES

SHOULDERS FOR CARRYIN' YE HOME WHEN YE MISSED YIZZER LAST BUS AN' CAN'T WALK ANYMORE

'MON, YOU'RE TAKIN' AGES' FACE

KEEPS ON WALKIN' EVEN IF YOU'RE A COUPLE OF MILES BEHIND. ME BOLLOX I'M RUNNIN' UP TO YE!

THE 'SICK OF WAITIN' ARM FOLD. HE DOES THE POXY SAME WHEN I'M SHOPPIN'

LONG LEGS FOR STRETCHIN' AN' WALKIN' FURTHER WITH. ME LEGS ARE ONLY HALF THE BLEEDIN' SIZE, STOP!

WALKS AT LEAST THREE STEPS FOR EVERY ONE STEP THA' YE TAKE

DOOR-TO-DOOR POXES

WHEN YOU'RE CHILLIN' OUT ABOUT TO WATCH SOMETHIN' ON THE AUL NETFLIX AN' THEN YE HAVE TO GET UP COS THE BLEEDIN' DOORBELL STARTS BUZZIN'. YE GO TO GET IT AN' IT'S SOME YOUNG FELLA TRYIN' TO SELL YE STUFF AN' ASKING, 'IS YOUR MAM OR DAD HOME?' THEY ALWAYS SAY THEY'LL CALL BACK AN' YOU'RE JUST THERE SAYIN' TO YIZZERSELF, 'PUSHY POX'. THIS IS HOW I DEAL WITH THE SAPS.

WHA' YE CAN DO

PULL YIZZER BLINDS DOWN SO THE POX THINKS THA' THERE'S NO ONE HOME AN' GOES AWAY.

SAY YOU'RE UNDER 18 AN' THEY LEGALLY CAN'T SELL YE ANYTHIN'. SORTED!

PUT A LOVELY SIGN UP IN YIZZER PORCH FOR THE CLOWNS.

TRY TO SELL THEM SOMETHIN' THA' YOU SELL OR A SERVICE YE PROVIDE.

POXES WHO ASK FOR A SMOKE

WHEN YOU'RE ENJOYIN' A SMOKE TO YIZZERSELF AN' SOME POX ASKS YE CAN YE LEAVE THEM AN END FOR THE FIFTIETH TIME AN' YOU'VE JUST HAD ENOUGH. LIKE, WHA'EVER HAPPENED TO WHEN YE WERE A KID AN' YE USED TO GIVE SOMEONE A EURDO FOR A SMOKE? THEY'RE NOT BLEEDIN' CHEAP ANYMORE, LIKE. BUY YOUR POXY OWN. HERE'S WHA' I DO WHEN SOME POX KEEPS ASKIN' ME FOR ONE AN' I'M NOT IN THE HUMOUR.

THE 'RECESSION SMOKE'

I LIKE TO CALL IT THE 'RECESSION SMOKE'. YE SHOULDN'T HAVE TO
HOOVER A SMOKE COS SOME POX IS RUSHIN' YE TO GIVE THEM AN
END. HERE'S WHA' YE DO.

YOU'VE JUST LIT ONE UP AN' SOMEONE'S ASKED
YE FOR AN END. YE SAY, 'YEAH, I'LL LEAVE YE
ONE IN A MINUTE'.

DON'T LOOK THEM IN THE EYE AN'
KEEP ON ENJOYIN' YIZZER SMOKE.

LEAVE THEM THE WRITIN'.

RACIST POXES

MAKE AMERICA POXY AGAIN, YE MEAN. YE MADE A BLEEDIN' MANDARIN YIZZER PRESIDENT!

HAS A BRAIN THE SIZE OF A LENTIL

SAGGY DIDDIES TRYIN' TO RUN AWAY FROM YE

IS RACIST BUT IRONICALLY HAS A TATTOO THAT'S BEEN APPROPRIATED FROM ANOTHER CULTURE

RUTHLESS FANNY PACK FULL OF HATE

SAY THEY WEAR ONLY AMERICAN-MADE CLOTHES ... THESE BOTTOMS WERE MADE IN CHINA

CAMEL-TOE CAVE OF HATE

POXES WHO START ON YE FOR NO REASON

I HATE IT WHEN YOUNG FELLAS AN' YOUNG WANS LOOK FOR FIGHTS
FOR NO REASON. LIKE SORRY, BUT WHA' THE HELL IS WRONG WITH
YE? THERE MUST BE SOMETHIN' UP IF YOU'RE THREATENIN' POXES
YE DON'T EVEN KNOW. GIVE IT OVER - YE DON'T LOOK LIKE A HARD
MAN YE LOOK LIKE A POXY FOOL CAUSIN' TROUBLE. IF YOU'RE A POX
WHO STARTS FIGHTS WITH PEOPLE FOR NO REASON, YOU'RE A TICK.

TRINITY POXES

BAG FULL OF WINE, COS TRINNERS POXES DON'T DRINK CANS WITH THE LADS

SMUG LOOK ON THEIR FACES

TRINITY JUMPER JUST IN CASE YE DIDN'T REALISE THA' THEY GO TO TRINITY

HOW DO YE KNOW IF SOMEONE GOES TO TRINITY? THEY POXY TELL YE! SWEAR, I'M SICK OF THESE TRINITY POXES THINKIN' THEY'RE BETTER THAN EVERYONE BLEEDIN' ELSE. JUST COS YOUR DA HAS FIVE BOATS AN' THE BANISTERS OF YIZZER STAIRS ARE MADE OUT OF RHINO HORN DOESN'T MAKE YE BETTER THAN ANYONE ELSE, PAL. STRUTTIN' AROUND WITH YIZZER TRINITY JUMPER LOOKIN' DOWN ON THE PEASANTS, GIVE ME A BLEEDIN' BREAK.

THE DIFFERENCE

THEY'RE BOTH HUMAN AN' SHIT FROM THE SAME HOLE.

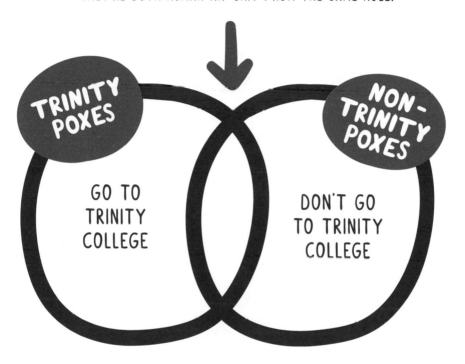

TRINITY POXES

NON-TRINITY POXES

GO TO TRINITY COLLEGE

DON'T GO TO TRINITY COLLEGE

GUESS WHA', PAL? YOU'RE NO MORE SPECIAL THAN ANYONE ELSE. DON'T GET ME WRONG, I'M SURE THERE'S SOME SOUND PEOPLE WHO GO TO TRINITY, BUT I HATE THE POXES WHO LOOK DOWN ON OTHERS AN' WERE BORN WITH A SILVER SPOON IN THEIR MOUTHS. YE GET NOWHERE IN LIFE WHEN YE LOOK DOWN ON PEOPLE. 'IT'S NICE TO BE IMPORTANT BUT IT'S IMPORTANT TO BE NICE.' - WISE AUL FELLA

IRISH HIPSTERS

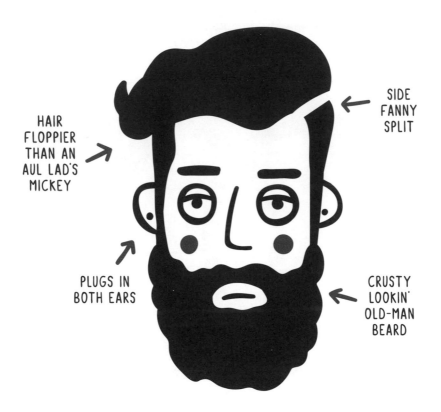

HAIR
FLOPPIER
THAN AN
AUL LAD'S
MICKEY

SIDE
FANNY
SPLIT

PLUGS IN
BOTH EARS

CRUSTY
LOOKIN'
OLD-MAN
BEARD

YE SEE THEM IN STONEYBATTER. YE SEE THEM IN YIZZER LOCAL SHOP. YE CAN'T EVEN GO FOR A COFFEE ANYMORE COS THEY'VE SHUT DOWN YIZZER LOCAL CAFÉ AN' OPENED THEIR OWN ONE THA' SELLS COFFEE SERVED IN POXY AVOCADOS. HERE'S HOW YE CAN DEAL WITH THE HIPSTER IN YIZZER AREA AN' HOW TO PISS THE POXES OFF.

WHA' TO DO

PUT A FEW BOTTLES OF IPA
OUTSIDE THE CAFÉ SO THEY'LL
ALL RUN OUT AN' THEN YE CAN
GET A SEAT.

ASK FOR MILK IN ONE OF THEIR
COFFEES AN' THEY'LL GO ON A
MAD ONE AT YE.

TELL THEM ABOUT A BAND THEY'VE
NEVER HEARD OF, BUT DON'T TELL
THEM IT'S FAKE.

TELL THEM YE CAN SEE NITS IN
THEIR BEARDS AN' THEY'LL START
SCREAMIN' THE GAFF DOWN.

PICK POCKETS IN TOWN

yoink!

THERE'S NOTHIN' WORSE THAN WHEN YE GO TO TAKE OUT YIZZER WALLET AN' YE REALISE THA' IT'S GONE. POXES WHO ROB FROM OTHER PEOPLE ARE THE LOWEST OF THE LOW. SWEAR, IF I CAUGH' ANYONE ROBBIN' FROM ME I'D GO ON AN' ABSOLUTE MAD ONE, I TELL YE. ALWAYS KEEP YIZZER BAG ZIPPED UP AN' PUT IT IN FRONT OF YE. AN' FOR THE LOVE OF GOD WILL YIZ STOP PUTTIN' YIZZER IPHONE IN YOUR BACK POCKET.

HOW TO PISS OFF A PICK POCKET

HERE'S HOW YE WRECK A PICK POCKET'S DAY, HUNS.

PUT A CACTUS IN YIZZER BAG FOR THE POX.

PUT THOSE MONEY NAPKINS FROM DEALZ IN YIZZER BAG.

PUT A BIG GREASY DILDO IN YIZZER BAG.

CARRY A NOKIA 3310 THA' DOESN'T WORK.

POXES
ONLINE

ALMOST EVERYONE THESE DAYS HAS A SMARTPHONE AN' A FACEBOOK ACCOUNT, WHICH MAKES IT MUCH MORE LIKELY THA' POXES WILL CREEP ONTO YIZZER TIMELINE. IN THIS CHAPTER I GIVE YE TIPS ON HOW TO DEAL WITH TROLLS, WHA' TO DO WHEN SOMEONE TAGS THEMSELVES IN THE HOSPITAL AN' WHA' I THINK OF POXES WHO SAY THEY HAVE A RIGH' TO THEIR OWN OPINION.

TYPES OF FACEBOOK POXES

YE DO MEET ALL KINDS OF PEOPLE ONLINE AN' MOST OF PEOPLE'S FACEBOOK PAGES ARE A COMBINATION OF OLD PRIMARY SCHOOL FRIENDS AN' FAKE PROFILES THA' THEY THOUGHT WERE REAL. HERE'S A FEW PEOPLE I'VE COME ACROSS ONLINE THA' I CAN SPOT A MILE AWAY NOW.

THE 'I HATE ALL MEN' POX

THE FELLA WHO THINKS HE'S MASSIVE

THE AUNTY WHO KEEPS POSTIN' ON YIZZER TIMELINE

THE WATERFORD WHISPERS BELIEVER

THE YOUNG WAN WITH LIP FILLERS

THE SHIT STIRRIN' POX

THE 'IS SHE FOR
REAL THINKIN' THAT'S
REAL?' SAP

THE CREEP WHO LOOKS
AT YOUR HOLIDAY PICS
FROM 2011

THE ACTIVIST POX

THE GRUMPY POX
WHO ALWAYS
GIVES OUT

THE 'I'M SO
OFFENDED'
POX

THE 'I'M ONLY
HERE FOR THE
COMMENTS' POX

THE JOURNAL
TROLL

THE CATFISH

THE MAM WHO
SHARES QUOTES

POXES WHO SHOW OFF

WHENEVER IT'S EASTER OR CHRISTMAS, PEOPLE ALWAYS COME OUT OF THE WOODWORK TO SHOW EVERYONE ON FACEBOOK WHA' THE EASTER BUNNY OR SANTY BROUGHT TO THEIR LOVELY LIL' PRINCES AN' PRINCESSES. I THINK IT'S A DISGRACE. THESE DAYS IT'S ALMOST LIKE A COMPETITION AS TO WHO GOT THE MOST. WHA' ABOUT THE KIDDIES WHO DIDN'T GET AS MUCH AS YOURS SEEIN' YOUR POST ON FACEBOOK? DON'T BE SHOWIN' OFF, YE LOOK LIKE A SAP.

WHA' HUNS THINK WHEN YE POST UP PICS

WHEN I SEE A YOUNG WAN POST UP PICS OF HOW SPOILED HER KIDDIE IS, NINE TIMES OUT OF TEN I EITHER BLOCK HER FROM ME NEWS FEED OR I END UP DELETIN' HER. THERE'S MORE TO LIFE THAN' FIDGET SPINNERS AN' IPADS, AN' YE SHOULD BE ENJOYIN' YIZZER TIME WITH YOUR KIDS INSTEAD OF LOOKIN' FOR LIKES ON FACEBOOK ALL THE TIME.

COULDN'T GIVE AN ACTUAL RAT'S

THA' CHILD IS FOUR AN' HAS A POXY IPAD

HATERS AN' TROLLS

THERE'S ALWAYS SOMEONE LURKIN' ON THE INTERNET WAITIN' TO
PUT SOMEONE DOWN WHEN THEY'RE DOIN' WELL FOR THEMSELVES
AN' WORKIN' HARD, OR A POX CYBERBULLYIN' SOMEONE. WHA' A SAD
LIFE' YIZ LEAD IF YE ONLY FEEL WHOLE WHEN YOU'RE DRAGGIN'
OTHERS DOWN. YE KNOW WHA' THEY SAY, HATERS GONNA HATE,
HUNS GONNA STUN. ON THE NEXT PAGE I SHOW YE HOW YE CAN
STAY HAPPY IN A WORLD OF INTERNET TROLLS.

HOW TO BE HAPPY

STAY WELL AWAY FROM THE
COMMENTS ON THE JOURNAL.

ACTUALLY, MAYBE JUST TURN OFF
YIZZER WIFI OR DATA.

ACTUALLY, TROW YIZZER PHONE
IN THE BIN, NEVER MIND THE WIFI.

GO OUT INTO THE REAL WORLD AN'
HAVE A LOOK AROUND YE.

HUNS WHO TAG THEMSELVES IN HOSPITAL

TAGS THEMSELVES IN HOSPITAL AS IF THEY WERE TAGGIN' THEMSELVES IN THE POXY AIRPORT

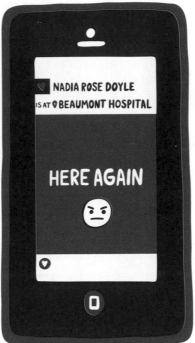

♥ NADIA ROSE DOYLE IS AT ⊙BEAUMONT HOSPITAL

HERE AGAIN

POSTS A PIC OF AN ANGRY EMOJI FOR SYMPATHY

SCROLLIN' THROUGH FACEBOOK YE ALWAYS COME ACROSS SOMEONE WHO'S TAGGED THEMSELVES IN HOSPITAL WITH NO EXPLANATION OF WHY THEY'RE THERE, SO EVERYONE STARTS ASKIN' THEM, 'ARE YE ALRI'?' AN' THEY'RE ALWAYS LIKE, 'I'M GRAND' ... THEN WHY POST IT? ATTENTION-SEEKIN' POXES. WHENEVER I SEE ANYONE DOIN' THIS I DO POST ONE OF THE COMMENTS THA' YE CAN SEE ON THE NEXT PAGE AN' THEY END UP LOOKIN' LIKE A SAP.

WHA' TO SAY TO THEM*

AH, IS IT YIZZER FANNY AGAIN?

DID YE GET THA' PILES CREAM SORTED, HUN?

YE OK, HUN?

YOUR MA TOLD ME ABOUT YIZZER NIPPLES

HOW DID YE GET THA' STUCK UP YIZZER ARSE?

* THEY MIGH' NOT TALK TO YE EVER AGAIN, JUST SO YE KNOW.

COMPETITION POXES

EVER GET A NOTIFICATION OR A MESSAGE AN' YE FEEL ALL POPULAR
BUT WHEN YE CLICK INTO IT IT'S SOMEONE LOOKIN' FOR YE TO
SHARE A COMPETITION FOR THEM TO WIN? EH, SORRY BUT WHY
WOULD I SHARE A COMPETITION FOR YE TO WIN A LOAD OF MAKE-UP
WHEN I CAN JUST TRY TO WIN IT MESELF? WRECKS ME HEAD.

YE SAY YE WILL
BUT YE NEVER DO

TYPES OF COMPETITION POXES

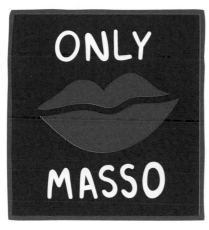

THE LIP-FILLER COMPETITIONS
FOR THE LIPLESS POXES.

THE LIBERAL.IE RIVER ISLAND
COMPETITIONS THA' NO ONE EVER
POXY WINS.

VOTE FOR ME BABY TO GET INTO
THE PAPERS WITH 500 OTHER
BABIES.

MUA HUN GIVEAWAYS FOR THE
MAKE-UP STUNNERS.

HASHTAG POXES

WHENEVER YE SEE SOMEONE USIN' A HASTAG ON FACEBOOK THEY ALWAYS USE IT FOR EVERY BLEEDIN' WORD IN THEIR SENTENCE. I'M GONNA SHOW YE HOW TO USE HASHTAGS AN' HOW TO GET THE BEST OF THEM, COS WHA' YOU'RE DOIN' MAKES NO BLEEDIN' SENSE, LUV. SORRY TO TELL YE.

A LESSON ON HASHTAGS

← THIS IS A HASHTAG

HASHTAGS WORK BETTER ON INSTA AN' TWITTER BECAUSE PEOPLE LOOK THEM UP TO FIND THINGS. SO FOR EXAMPLE, IF YE HAVE #BEACH, LOADS OF PICTURES OF BEACHES COME UP AN' YOURS WILL BE THERE TOO. THAT'S HOW YE DRAW ATTENTION TO YIZZER PAGE, NOT BY SAYIN':
#ME #SON #IS
#ME #WORLD

THE 'THAT'S MY OPINION' TYPE OF POX

FACE ON THEM
LIKE SOMEONE
PISSED IN THEIR
CORN FLAKES

WON'T STOP GOIN'
ON UNTIL THEY
HAVE THE LAST
WORD AN' WANT
YE TO GO WITH
THEIR OPINION

SOMETIMES
SO SCARY THA'
YOU'RE NOT SURE IF
THEY'RE CARRYIN'
A BLADE AN' KNOW
WHERE YE LIVE

THE 'SHIT JUST
GOT SERIOUS'
ARM POSE -
USUALLY USED
AFTER SOMEONE
QUESTIONS THEIR
OPINION AN' THEY
CAN'T BACK IT UP

GIVE IT
BLEEDIN' OVER

PLZ JUST STOP

EVERYONE 'HAS A RIGH' TO THEIR OWN OPINION' THESE DAYS AN'
THAT'S ALL WELL AN' GOOD, BUT THERE'S SOMETHIN' YE SHOULD
KNOW. JUST COS IT'S YOUR OPINION DOESN'T MAKE IT THE RIGH'
OPINION, AN' IT SURE AS HELL DOESN'T MEAN PEOPLE HAVE TO
AGREE WITH YE. SO TAKE YIZZER CLAWS BACK IN AN' NEXT TIME
SOMEONE QUESTIONS YE ON YOUR OPINION, AT LEAST BE ABLE TO
BACK UP WHA' YE SAID. OTHERWISE YE LOOK LIKE A SPA, HUN.

SELFIE POXES

WE ALL HAVE ONE FRIEND WHO POSTS UP PICTURES OF THE NIGH'
BEFORE WITHOUT SHOWIN' YE THEM FIRST, AN' NINE TIMES OUT OF
TEN THEY LOOK UNREAL AN' YOU LOOK ROTTEN. I'M NOT GONNA LIE,
I DO THIS ALL THE TIME. WHEN TANYA GETS HER DRINK ON, HER
EYES START GOIN' ALL OVER THE PLACE AN' YE DON'T EVEN KNOW
WHEN THE POX IS TALKIN' TO YE.

THE HUN FILTER

LIL' CHEETAH
EARS ON YE

GRAND FOR
CONTOURIN'

SEE YE LATER,
DOUBLE CHIN

IN SAYIN' THA', TANYA SWEARS BY THE CHEETAH HUN FILTER. YE
SEE WHEN YOU'RE LOCKED AN' YE LOOK ROTTEN AT THE END OF
THE NIGH'? IT MAKES YE LOOK MASSIVE AGAIN, SWEAR. IT'S LIKE
SOME KIND OF HARRY POTTER MAGIC OR SOMETHIN'. DON'T KNOW
HOW IT WORKS BUT I'M NOT COMPLAININ' COS IT HAS ME LOOKIN'
PURE STUNNIN' ON A DAILY BASIS.

ARE YE A HATER?

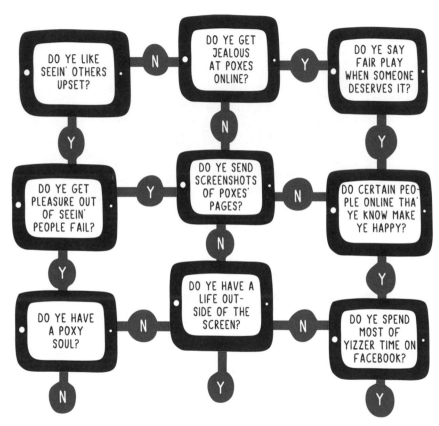

DO YE LIKE SEEIN' OTHERS UPSET?

DO YE GET JEALOUS AT POXES ONLINE?

DO YE SAY FAIR PLAY WHEN SOMEONE DESERVES IT?

DO YE GET PLEASURE OUT OF SEEIN' PEOPLE FAIL?

DO YE SEND SCREENSHOTS OF POXES' PAGES?

DO CERTAIN PEOPLE ONLINE THA' YE KNOW MAKE YE HAPPY?

DO YE HAVE A POXY SOUL?

DO YE HAVE A LIFE OUTSIDE OF THE SCREEN?

DO YE SPEND MOST OF YIZZER TIME ON FACEBOOK?

CONGRATULATIONS! YOU'RE THE ULTIMATE BEGRUDGER. YE HATE TO SEE ANYONE DOIN' WELL FOR THEMSELVES AN' YE LEAD A SAD LIFE.

YE PRAISE YIZZER FRIENDS WHEN THEY DO WELL AN' YE SHOW THEM HOW PROUD YE ARE. YE ALSO LIKE TO SPEND TIME OFFLINE IN THE REAL WORLD.

YOU ALSO HAVE TIME FOR YIZZER MATES. YE SPEND MOST OF YIZZER TIME ONLINE CHATTIN' TO NEW PEOPLE AN' MAKIN' NEW FRIENDS.

WHA' ARE YE LIKE ONLINE?

MONTH YE WERE BORN

FIRST LETTER OF YIZZER NAME

JAN ANNOYIN'
FEB STRANGE
MAR BALLBAG
APR SNAPCHAT
MAY BUZZ WRECKIN'
JUN FUN SUCKIN'
JUL COMMENT READIN'
AUG WEIRDO
SEP SCARY
OCT GEEBAG
NOV FACEBOOK
DEC INSTA

A HOOP HATER
B TROLL TEASER
C MEME WANKER
D PICTURE CREEPER
E CAT FANATIC
F PHONE LICKER
G STALKER SAP
H PEEPIN' POX
I NOSEY SAP
J INTERNET CREEP
K JOURNAL TROLL
L VIDEO WATCHER
M BLOGGIN' SAP

N FOOD SNAPPER
O CAMEL LOVER
P RUNNER SCRUBBER
Q COMPETITION SAP
R MOANER
S HACKER
T SMOOTH SCROLLER
U SILENT STALKER
V VIRAL QUEEN
W PORN WATCHIN' POX
X OPINION HOLDER
Y SCREEN SCROLLER
Z ATTENTION SEEKER

POXES
IN THE CLUB

SEE WHEN IT TURNS FRIDAY? I DO BE BUZZIN' TO GET OUT FOR A BOP
WITH THE GIRLS, BUT THERE'S ALWAYS SOMEONE WHO TRIES TO RUIN YOUR
POXY NIGH'. THIS CHAPTER GOES THROUGH EVERYTHIN' FROM POXES YE
SEE ON A NIGH' OUT TO BOUNCERS BEIN' TICKS FOR NO REASON AN' HOW
TO DEAL WITH THEM.

TYPES OF POXES YE SEE ON A NIGH' OUT

WHEN YE GO INTO TOWN AT NIGH' YE DO COME ACROSS ALL KINDS OF PEOPLE. SWEAR! SOME ARE MAD SOUND AN' SOME ARE ABSOLUTE WEIRDOS, I TELL YE. THESE ARE SOME OF THE POXES I COME ACROSS WHEN I GO TO THE CLUB WITH THE GIRLS.

THE POX WHOSE
EYELASH IS
ESCAPIN'

THE FUCK BOY
IN THE TANK TOP

THE ONE WHO TOOK
ALL DAY TO GET READY

THE FELLA WHO'S
CLEARLY ON YOKES

THE YOUNG WAN
WHO'S ONLY 16

THE CREEP
WHO KEEPS
STAIRIN' AT YE

POXES WHO TELL YE HOW
MANY SYNS ARE IN YIZZER DRINK

ME FRIEND STEPHANIE IS ALWAYS TELLIN' ME HOW MANY SYNS ARE IN ME POXY DRINK. I'M OUT TO ENJOY MESELF AN' NOT THINK ABOUT SLIMMIN' WORLD. LIKE, LET'S BE HONEST, I'M GONNA HAVE A CHICKEN FILLET ROLL AN' A SPICEBAG THE NEXT DAY WHEN I'M DYIN', SO A LIL' VODKA AN' COKE WON'T HURT, HUN.

POXES WHO WALK ALL OVER YE

WHEN YOU'RE DANCIN' AN' YOU'RE HAVIN' THE TIME OF YIZZER LIFE,
BOPPIN' AWAY TO A BIT OF THE BRUNO, AN' SOME YOKE STANDS
ON YIZZER FOOT AN' NEARLY BREAKS THE THING! NOTHIN' WORSE,
ESPECIALLY WHEN THEY KEEP DOIN' IT TO YE COS THEY'RE FALLIN'
ALL OVER THE GAFF. HERE'S HOW I COPE WITH THESE POXES.

HOW TO GET THEM BACK

WEAR A SIGN SO TALL PEOPLE KNOW THA' YOU'RE STANDIN' THERE AN' NOT TO WALK ON YE.

POUR HALF A CAN OF DUTCH IN THEIR POCKET WHEN THEY'RE NOT LOOKIN' AN' THEY'LL MOVE.

IF IT'S A FELLA YE CAN TELL HIM TO STOP OR HE'LL GET A HEADBUTT IN THE BALL SACK.

STAND ON THEM BACK AN' THEY'LL KNOW ALL ABOUT IT.

WHEN YE CAN'T REACH THE BAR

THIS YOKE HERE.
LIFESAVER, SWEAR!

YE EVER STAND AT THE BAR WAITIN' TO GET A DRINK AN' THE BAR
MAN CAN'T EVEN SEE YE, AN' YE KEEP WAVIN' AT HIM BUT THERE'S
SOME TALL POX BLOCKIN' YIZZER WAY? I ALWAYS STAND ON THE LIL'
FOOT BAR SO THEY CAN SEE YE. IT GIVES YE AT LEAST ANOTHER
FOOT AN' YE CAN GET YIZZER DRINK FASTER. IT ALWAYS WORKS
FOR ME IN ANYWAY. BEST INVENTION EVER.

TYPES OF SHOES ON NIGHTS OUT

IF THERE'S ONE THING THA' WILL GRAB SOMEONE'S ATTENTION ON A NIGH' OUT, IT'S A GOOD SHOE. YE CAN NEVER GO WRONG WITH A NICE PAIR OF HEELS. ANTO DOES GO MAD AT ME COS IT'S ALL I SPEND ME MONEY ON THESE DAYS. SOMETIMES POXES WEAR MAD SHIT OUT. THESE ARE SOME OF THE SHOES I'VE SEEN IN ACTUAL CLUBS.

HEELS THA' ARE
DEARER THAN
YIZZER GAFF

WINTER BOOTS
WITH TIGHTS

BOSS YOUNG
WAN HEELS

KITTEN HEELS PAIRED
WITH A JUMPSUIT - WHA'
EVEN IS THA'?

PUMPS WHEN YIZZER
FEET ARE KILLIN' YE

HOW THE HELL DID
YE GET PAST THE
BOUNCERS, PAL,
SERIOUSLY?

BOUNCER POXES

THE FEAR THA' YE GET WHEN YOU'RE WAITIN' IN LINE TO GET INTO A CLUB AN' THE BOUNCER IS GOIN' ON A PURE POWER TRIP, GRILLIN' EVERYONE IN THE LINE ON WHA' THEIR STAR SIGN IS AN' LETTIN' THEM IN BASED ON HOW THEY'RE DRESSED. SOME BOUNCERS ARE POXES BUT SOME ARE ACTUALLY ALRIGH'. I GOT SICK ON ONE ONCE AN' HE LET ME BACK IN LATER THA' NIGH' WHEN I WAS GRAND AGAIN.

TIPS FOR GETTIN' IN

KNOW WHA' YIZZER DATE OF BIRTH AN' STAR SIGN IS JUST IN CASE.

LOOK THEM DEAD IN THE EYE AN' TELL THEM YOU'RE DEFO SOBER.

DON'T TRY TO GET IN WITH A SHITTY ID COS THEY KNOW FULL WELL, LUV.

HIDE A NAGGIN SOMEWHERE THEY WOULD NEVER THINK, LIKE IN YIZZER HUN BUN.

POXES WHO ROB YIZZER DRINK

YE SEE WHEN YE GET A NEW DRINK AN' SOME POX IS WATCHIN'
YE, WAITIN' FOR YE TO MOVE SO THEY CAN TAKE YIZZER DRINK
FROM THE TABLE? BUY YIZZER OWN DRINKS, YE CRUSTY ANIMALS.
I WORKED ALL WEEK SO I CAN AFFORD TO GO OUT AN' SPEND ME
MONEY, AN' THE LAST THING I WANT IS SOME GEEBAG ROBBIN' ALL
ME DRINKS FROM THE TABLE. SAPS.

DRINKS FOR POXES

THESE ARE THE TOP DRINKS YE DO SEE POXES DRINKIN'
NOWADAYS OUT IN THE CLUBS AN' PUBS.

SHOTS FOR THE MAD YOKES
OUT FOR THE NIGH'

GIN AN' TONIC FOR
THE HEALTH FREAKS

HALF PINTS FOR THE
EARLY RISERS

COCKTAILS FOR THE HUNS

TOILET HOGGIN' POXES

WHEN YOU'RE BURSTIN' TO GO TOILET AN' SOME POXES ARE TAKIN' AGES IN THERE AN' THEY DON'T EVEN NEED TO GO THEMSELVES, COS YE CAN SEE ABOUT SIX LEGS UNDER THE JAYSUSIN' DOOR. HAVE YIZZER LIL' HEART TO HEART IN THE POXY SMOKIN' AREA, LUV, COS I ACTUALLY NEED TO GO. SWEAR, SOMETIMES I WISH I WERE A FELLA. THEY'RE JUST IN AN' OUT OF THE TOILET, NO MESSIN' AROUND WITH THEM. IF YE DON'T SPEND HALF YIZZER NIGH' WAITIN' TO GO TOILET, ARE YE EVEN IN A CLUB AT ALL?

REASONS POXES TAKE AGES IN THE TOILET

SWIPIN' ON TINDER FOR
TWO HOURS STRAIGH'

SOBBIN' OVER FELLAS

TOOK A SHIT AN' RAN
OUT OF JAX ROLL

WATCHIN' THE
CORONATION STREET
POXY OMNIBUS

WHEN YOUR BESTO IS SOBBIN'

HE'S MEETIN' A YOUNG WAN WHO LOOKS LIKE A POXY CAMEL

SOMETIMES IT'S YOU WHO'S IN THE JAX FOR AGES WITH YIZZER FRIEND AN' SHE'S PURE SOBBIN' OVER A FELLA WHO'S AFTER GOIN' AN' BREAKIN' HER HEART. SOMETIMES IT'S OVER NOTHIN' AN' YOU'RE JUST LIKE, 'WILL YE COME ON!' YE DO FEEL BAD FOR THEM AN' ALL, BUT AT THE SAME TIME YE DO KEEP CHECKIN' YIZZER PHONE BECAUSE YE KNOW IT'S GETTIN' CLOSE TO LAST ORDERS AN' YOU'RE NOT EVEN READY TO GO HOME YET.

WHA' YE CAN DO

WHEN ONE OF ME FRIENDS IS PURE SOBBIN' IN THE JAX THERE'S ONLY TWO THINGS YE CAN DO TO GET THEM BACK OUT THERE ENJOYIN' THEMSELVES. IF ALL ELSE FAILS, THERE'S NOTHIN' YE CAN REALLY DO OTHER THAN LEAVE, WHICH IS POXY, BUT MAKIN' SURE YIZZER FRIEND IS OK IS WAY MORE IMPORTANT THAN A JAGER BOMB, HUN.

LISTEN TO WHA' THEY HAVE TO SAY. BE A GOOD FRIEND, BUT IF THEY'RE TALKIN' A LOAD OF BOLLOX SAY, 'STOP THA', YOU'RE ONLY UPSETTIN' YIZZERSELF EVEN MORE'. TRY AN' GET THEM TO GO BACK OUT AN' ENJOY THEMSELVES FOR THE REST OF THE NIGH'. YE ONLY LIVE ONCE AN' ALL.

IF IT'S ABOUT A FELLA, TELL HER THA' SHE CAN DO WAY BETTER AN' THA' HE'S A PIG. SHE DOESN'T NEED THA' KIND OF POX RUININ' HER LIFE AN' WRECKIN' HER HEAD. DELETE HIS NUMBER, BLOCK HIM AND MOVE ON. THERE'S PLENTY OF NICE YOUNG FELLAS FLOATIN' ABOUT.

WHEN YIZZER MATE IS PURE LOCKED

WE ALL HAVE THA' ONE FRIEND WHO GOES IN TOO HARD AT THE
START OF THE NIGH' AN' DOES BE LOCKED BY 12 O'CLOCK. THE ONLY
THING YE CAN DO IF YIZZER FRIEND IS THA' BAD IS BRING THE POX
FOR FOOD AN' TRY TO SOBER THEM UP. WRECKS ME HEAD WHEN
THEY START RUNNIN' OFF ON YE. HUN, I DON'T WORK IN A CRÈCHE.
COP ON AN' GET THOSE CHICKEN NUGGETS INTO YE.

BRING THEM TO MCDONALD'S

SCREW SLIMMIN' WORLD'S
BIG MAC IN A BOWL.
THIS IS FUCKIN' MASSIVE!

NOTHIN' TASTES BETTER THAN A MCDONALD'S AT THE END OF THE NIGH'. THE FOOD COULD HAVE BEEN MADE FIVE HOURS AGO AN' YE STILL COULDN'T GIVE A RAT'S COS IT TASTES THA' GOOD WHEN YOU'VE BEEN OUT ALL NIGH' DRINKIN'. THE ONLY THING THA' WRECKS ME HEAD IS THE QUEUES IN THE POXY PLACE. I DO ALWAYS SKIP THEM AN' GO UP TO SOME RANDOMER LIKE, 'AH MARTINA, THANKS FOR SAVIN' ME SPOT, HUN'. WORKS ALL THE TIME FOR ME AN' TANYA.

THE SNAP CHAT FEAR

WHEN YE WAKE UP THE NEXT MORNIN' IN BITS TO WHATSAPP GROUP MESSAGES ABOUT WHA' YE DID LAST NIGH' AN' THA' DREADED QUESTION, 'DID YE SEE YIZZER SNAP CHAT STORY?' WELL NO, I DIDN'T. I'M ONLY BLEEDIN' UP AN' THE THING HAS 800 VIEWS. NEVER BRINGIN' ME PHONE OUT WITH ME AGAIN, SWEAR. DO BE SCARLEH SOMETIMES LOOKIN' BACK AT IT.

ARE YE A SAP WHEN YOU'RE LOCKED?

YOU'RE A GOOD MATE. YOUS ALL STICK TOGETHER AN' HAVE A GREAT NIGH' AN' GET HOME SAFE AN' ALL.

YOU'RE A SAP. YE END UP RUININ' EVERYONE ELSE'S NIGH' BY DRINKIN' TOO MUCH. CALM DOWN AN' DON'T POXY DRINK AS MUCH BEFORE YE HEAD OUT.

YOU'RE NOT A SAP, YE JUST LIKE TO HAVE A GOOD TIME. ONCE YE DON'T LOSE YIZZER MATES YOU'RE GRAND, HUN.

POXES
ON THE ROAD

THERE'S ALWAYS SOME SORT OF POX OUT ON THE ROADS, WHETHER IT'S A TICK WHO KEEPS BEEPIN' AT YE FOR NO REASON OR A CYCLIST JUST MINDIN' THEIR OWN BUSINESS CYCLIN' IN THE MIDDLE OF THE POXY ROAD. THIS CHAPTER GOES THROUGH EVERYTHIN', FROM DUBLIN ROADKILL AN' ROAD SIGNS TO MOAN-BAG TAXI DRIVERS AN' MORE.

IRISH ROAD
SURVIVAL KIT

THIS IS ME IRISH ROAD SURVIVAL KIT. IF YE HAVE ONE OF THESE, YOU'LL BE GRAND ON THE ROAD. NOT A BOTHER ON YE, PAL.

MAGIC MIRROR SO YE
CAN SEE CYCLISTS
COMIN' AROUND CORNERS.

STRESS BALL WHEN
YE CAN'T DEAL WITH
THE TRAFFIC GOIN'
INTO THE OMNI.

WATER GUN FULL OF
HOT SAUCE FOR POXES
WHO START ON YE.

A CAMERA THA' TELLS
YE WHEN THERE'S A
CHECKPOINT COMIN' UP.

DUBLIN ROADKILL

SOME OF THE ROADKILL I'VE SEEN IN DUBLIN OVER THE YEARS. YE HAVE TO BE SOME SICK ANIMAL TO RUN OVER A SPICEBAG.

TRAFFIC CONE

LOST SHOE WITH
KEBAB SAUCE

A POOR
SPICEBAG

THE HEEL OFF
A SLICED PAN

THE TYRE OFF
A ROBBED BIKE

A VOTIN' SIGN
ON THE M50

POXES ON BIKES

TIP: PUT A PLASTIC BOTTLE HERE SO IT MAKES A MO-TORBIKE SOUND AN' PEOPLE WILL THINK YOU'RE ON A HARLEY-DAVIDSON.

OVER THE LAST COUPLE OF YEARS, EVERYONE IS HOPPIN' UP ON THEIR BIKES THINKIN' THEY'RE LIKE YOUR MAN LANCE ARMSTRONG OR SOMETHIN', BOMBIN' IT AROUND TOWN. BUT WHA' SOME OF THE SAPS DON'T REALISE IS THA' THERE'S A BIG DIFFERENCE BETWEEN CYCLIN' AROUND A CUL DE SAC WHEN YOU'RE TEN AND CYCLIN' ON A MAIN ROAD WITH CARS AN' BUSES. SOME OF THEM ARE MAD BASTARDS.

HOW TO NOT DIE
(IF YOU'RE A CYCLIST)

IF YE WANT TO HAVE A SAFE CYCLE AN' MAKE IT TO WORK ALIVE, DO ALL OF THE THINGS BELOW AN' YOU'LL BE GRAND. IT WON'T STOP YE FROM GETTIN' A SMACK, BUT IT COULD PREVENT YE FROM GETTIN' ONE, IF YE KNOW WHA' I MEAN.

A HELMET TO SAVE
YE FROM CRACKIN'
YIZZER HEAD.

A HI-VIS SO EVERYONE
CAN SEE YE IN THE
POXY DARK.

WATCH OUT FOR
THE CARS, OBVIOUSLY.

DON'T BE CYCLIN' AROUND
LIKE MISS DAISY ON A
MAIN ROAD.

MOAN-BAG TAXI DRIVERS

HE CAN HEAR YE TALKIN' BUT DOESN'T GIVE A RAT'S

HAS A FACE LIKE A MELTED YANKEE CANDLE

EVERYONE AT LEAST ONCE IN THEIR ACTUAL LIFE COMES ACROSS A MOAN-BAG TAXI DRIVER. THE KIND OF FELLA WHO DOESN'T GIVE A RAT'S AN' IS GRUMPY WITH YE THE WHOLE POXY JOURNEY. LISTEN, PAL, THIS IS YOUR JOB. YE PROVIDE A BLEEDIN' SERVICE! DON'T BE TAKIN' IT OUT ON ME IF YOU'VE BEEN WAITIN' AT THE OMNI FOR THREE HOURS AN' I WANT TO GET A LIFT BACK TO MY ANTO'S AN' THE FARE IS ONLY A FIVER. GERRRUP!

TYPES OF TAXI DRIVERS

IN SAYIN' THA', THANK FUCK THERE'S MORE SOUND TAXI DRIVERS
OUT THERE THAN THERE ARE MOAN BAGS: THE KIND OF DRIVERS
WHO ARE UP FOR A LAUGH AN' SOMETIMES CAN EVEN MAKE YIZZER
DAY. THESE ARE THE FELLAS WHO DON'T GET ENOUGH PRAISE FOR
WHA' THEY DO. HERE'S TO ALL THE SOUND TAXI DRIVERS OUT THERE.

THE ONE WHO
WAITS UNTIL HE
SEES YE GETTIN'
IN SAFELY

THE ONE WHO STOPS
THE METER IF YOU'RE
STUCK IN TRAFFIC

THE ONE WHO
CHATS WITH YE
THE WHOLE TIME

THE ONE WHO
HATES RACIST
TAXI DRIVERS

THE ONE WHO
KNOWS ALL THE
BEST SHORTCUTS

THE ONE WHO HAS
MAD STORIES TO
TELL YE

POXES WITH ROAD RAGE

WHEN YOU'RE MINDIN' YIZZER OWN BUSINESS AN' SOME ABSOLUTE SPA STARTS GOIN' ON A MAD ONE AT YE FOR NOT LETTIN' THEM OUT. ME AN' ANTO GOT CHASED THROUGH PHIBSBORO BEFORE AN' I WAS SOBBIN. I WAS LIKE TO MESELF, 'THIS IS HOW YOU'RE GONNA DIE, IN A POXY CIVIC'. I CALLED THE GARDAÍ AN' ALL! WAS TERRIFYIN'. POXES NEED TO CALM DOWN COS IT DOESN'T SOLVE ANYTHIN'. TICKS.

ANATOMY
OF THE FINGER

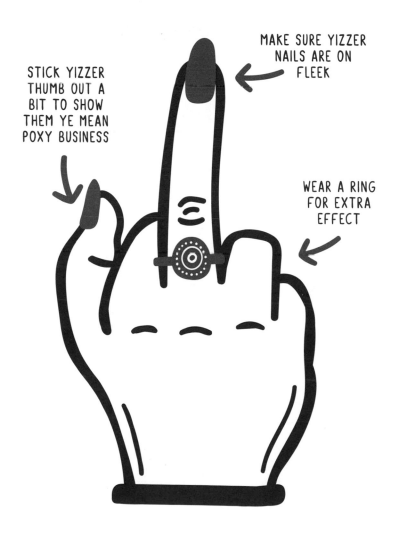

MAKE SURE YIZZER
NAILS ARE ON
FLEEK

STICK YIZZER
THUMB OUT A
BIT TO SHOW
THEM YE MEAN
POXY BUSINESS

WEAR A RING
FOR EXTRA
EFFECT

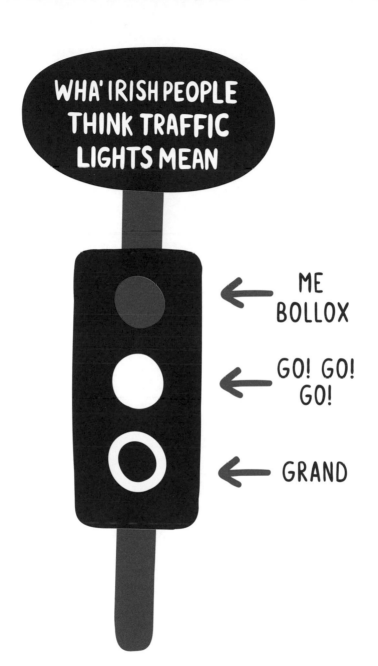

LIGH' PRESSIN' POXES

PUT SOME
KETCHUP ON
THE BUTTON

DO YE EVER BE IN A RUSH SOMEWHERE AN' SOME POX KEEPS PRESSIN' THE BUTTON AT THE LIGHTS AN' THEN WHEN NOTHIN' IS COMIN' THEY CROSS ANYWAY? THEN YOU'RE LEFT WAITIN' IN THE CAR AT THE LIGHTS SWEATIN' TO GET TO THE CREDIT UNION. THERE'S ONLY ONE WAY TO GET THESE POXES BACK AN' THAT'S BY PUTTIN' SOMETHIN' ON THE BUTTON THA' THEY'RE LEAST EXPECTIN'.

POXES WHO PUT BUGGIES OUT ON THE ROAD

EH, HELLO? THIS IS YOUR BABY, YE KNOW THE THING THA' YOUS WAITED NINE MONTHS TO HAVE?

NOTHIN' WRECKS ME HEAD MORE THAN SEEIN' YOUNG WANS AN' YOUNG FELLAS WITH THEIR BUGGIES OUT ON THE ROAD WAITIN' ON THE LIGHTS. YIZ DO REALISE THA' NOT EVERYONE IS A GOOD DRIVER? DON'T BE PUTTIN' YIZZER PRAMS OUT ON THE ROAD COS GOD KNOWS WHA' COULD HAPPEN. I JUST DON'T GET WHA' DOES BE GOIN' THROUGH PEOPLE'S HEADS SOMETIMES. I SEEN ANTO'S MA DOIN' IT BEFORE BUT SHE ONLY HAD SUPERVALU BAGS IN IT SO THA' WAS GRAND.

ROAD SIGNS

MY ANTO IS A BRILLIANT DRIVER, SWEAR. I DON'T KNOW HOW HE DOES IT SOMETIMES. THE BLEEDIN' STRESS OF IT WITH ALL THE SAPS WHO CAN'T DRIVE ON THE ROAD, LIKE. THIS IS A LIST OF ALL THE ROAD SIGNS IN IRELAND. THINK OF THIS YOKE AS YIZZER OWN PERSONAL MANUAL, HUN. IF YOU'RE PRACTISIN' FOR YIZZER THEORY TEST, THIS IS PERFECT! YOU'LL PASS WITH FLYIN' COLOURS.

CAN'T TAKE A LEFT, BUT YE CAN IF NO ONE'S LOOKIN'

SAYS 30 BUT YE CAN PROB GO 40, LIKE

YOUR FELLA WHEN YE START TALKIN' ABOUT GETTIN' MARRIED

YOUR FELLA EVERY MORNIN'

POXES CROSSIN' WHEN THEY'RE LOCKED

PARK HERE AN' YOU'RE A DEAD MAN

KEEP AN' EYE OUT
FOR THE TRAMPS IN
THIS AREA

KIDDIES MORE THAN
LIKELY TO RUN OUT
IN FRONT OF YE

WHEN YE HAVE TO
WORK STEPHEN'S DAY

SELFIE PIT STOP
FOR THE STUNNERS

WHEN SOMEONE
SAYS THEY DON'T
LIKE NUGGETS

WARNIN', SNAKES
AHEAD, WATCH
YIZZER BACKS

POXES NOT
ALLOWED IN

HOW YIZZER HEAD
FEELS AFTER A NIGH'
OUT

DIDDIE RAMPS

135

WHEN YE HAVEN'T GOT A CAR TO GO THROUGH THE DRIVE THRU

IF YE DON'T HAVE YIZZER OWN CAR AN' THE QUEUE IN MCDONALD'S IS HUGE, HERE'S A LIST OF THINGS YE CAN USE INSTEAD OF A CAR FOR YIZZER VERY OWN DRIVE THRU EXPERIENCE. SOMETIMES TANYA DOES GO IN ON A BARBIE SCOOTER AN' THEY SERVE HER NO BOTHER. ME BOLLOX I'M ORDERIN' INSIDE, THE QUEUE IS BLEEDIN' MENTAL.

A WHEELIE BIN

A UNICYCLE

A HOVERBOARD

A HORSE

A WHEELBARROW

YOUR NANNY'S
SCOOTER

THINGS YE FIND IN YIZZER CAR

COFFEE CUP WITH COLD COFFEE

THE FAMOUS 'LOOSE MCDONALD'S CHIP'

AIR FRESHENER THAT'S THREE YEARS OLD

HELP!

CRUMBS FROM FUCK KNOWS WHA' - ANIMALS HAVE THE CAR IN BITS

TAKEAWAY BAGS LEFT IN THE CAR

HOW MUCH OF A POXY DRIVER ARE YOU?

POXES
ON HOLIDAY

WHEN IT'S THE SUMMER AN' YOU'RE DYIN' TO GET AWAY AN' GET A BIT OF SUN, SOMETHIN' ALWAYS TENDS TO WRECK YIZZER BUZZ OR GO WRONG. THIS CHAPTER GOES THROUGH EVERYTHIN' YE NEED TO KNOW, FROM HOW TO GET POXES TO STOP SNORIN' TO WHEN YIZZER DIDDIES ARE SWEATIN' IN 40-DEGREE HEAT AN' YE CAN'T COPE ANYMORE.

POXES WHO PUT UP PRE-HOLIDAY PICS

NEW HAIRCUT BEFORE YIZZER HOLLIERS

THE 'HUN' POSE - REST YIZZER ARM ON YOUR HIP FOR FULL EFFECT

STAND IN FRONT OF YIZZER MIRROR TO TAKE THE SELFIE

I ALWAYS PUT UP A PRE-HOLIDAY PIC OF ME NEW BIKINI AN' ALL AN' SAY SOMETHIN' LIKE, 'ONLY ONE MORE WEEK, BENIDORM WON'T KNOW WHA' HIT IT'. TANYA IS ALWAYS SAYIN' I LOOK LIKE A SAP PUTTIN' UP A PIC OF MESELF IN A BIKINI IN ME ROOM. SHE DOES SAY SOMETHIN' ON ME STATUS LIKE, 'EH, YE DO KNOW YE CAN SEE YIZZER KNICKERS ON THE FLOOR IN THA' PIC?' HERE'S A LIST OF THINGS I DO BEFORE ME HOLLIERS.

HOLIDAY POX
STARTER PACK

FLIP FLOPS FROM PENNEYS SO
YE DON'T GET VERRUCAS.
THEY'RE POXY ROTTEN.

THE COUNTDOWN CALENDAR ON ME
PHONE. ONLY 5 MONTHS, 3 DAYS,
23 HOURS AN' 15 MINUTES TO GO.

I ALWAYS PACK WAY TOO MUCH AN'
DON'T EVEN WEAR HALF THE POXY
THINGS.

GET A GOOD SET OF ACRYLICS
A COUPLE OF DAYS BEFORE YE
GO AWAY. MASSIVE!

WHEN YIZZER DIDDIES SWEAT

THE RIVER BLEEDIN' LIFFEY, SWEAR!

IF YE HAVE BIG DIDDIES YOU'LL KNOW THE STRUGGLE. IF YE DON'T THEN YOU'RE LUCKY ENOUGH TO LIVE A CARE-FREE LIFE AN' YOU'LL KNOW ALL ABOUT IT WHEN YOU'RE 60 OR SOMETHIN' AND THEY'RE SAGGY AS FUCK. I TELL YE, THERE'S NOTHIN' WORSE THAN WHEN YOU'RE ON HOLIDAY AN' YOU'RE MINDIN' YIZZER OWN BUSINESS AN' THEY JUST START SWEATIN' AN' STICKIN' TOGETHER. HERE'S WHA' I DO TO KEEP THEM FROM DRIPPIN' ALL OVER THE GAFF.

LIFE SAVERS

REALLY DOES WORK, I'M NOT TAKIN' THE PISS

ROLL ON

BITTA ROLL-ON DEODORANT IS A LIFE SAVER, SWEAR! YOU'LL BE SURPRISED, AN' IT WORKS GOOD FOR CHAFING AS WELL. THE PANTY LINER IS ANOTHER GOOD ONE IF YE PUT THEM IN THE AREA THAT'S BOTHERIN' YE. SOMETIMES I STICK THEM TO THE ARMPITS OF ME DRESS AN' NO ONE CAN EVEN SEE, SO WHEN YOU'RE HAVIN' A HOLIDAY BOP NO ONE KNOWS THA' YOU'RE SWEATIN'. ME FRIEND MELISSA SHOWED ME THA' LIL' TRICK.

WHEN YE GET RIPPED OFF

YE EVER GO AWAY AN' SOME FELLA TRIES TO GET YE TO GO INTO
HIS RESTAURANT COS IT'S 'THE BEST ON THE STRIP'? SO YE GO IN
AN' THE POX CHARGES YE THROUGH THE POXY ROOF! YE CAN AVOID
THESE PLACES BY NOT GOIN' IN, OBVIOUSLY. HOW YE CAN SPOT
THEM IS EASY. IF A FELLA IS TRYIN' TO GET YE TO GO IN SAYIN',
'GREAT FOOD, GREAT COCKTAILS', DON'T DO IT, COS NINE TIMES OUT
OF TEN IT'S A LOAD OF BOLLOX IF I'M BEIN' PURE HONEST WITH YE.

WHEN THERE'S NO KETTLE IN YIZZER ROOM

HAVIN' NO KETTLE CAN CAUSE RUCTIONS, I TELL YE

ON TRIPADVISOR IT SAID THA' YOU'D HAVE A KETTLE IN YIZZER ROOM, BUT WHEN YE ARRIVE THERE'S NO SIGN OF ONE COS WHA' IRISH PERSON WOULD WANT TO BE DRINKIN' TEA WHEN THEY'RE POXY AWAY? I DO ALWAYS BRING A LIL' TRAVEL KETTLE WITH ME WHEN I'M GOIN' ON HOLIDAYS JUST IN CASE, COS IF I DON'T GET ME CUP OF TEA FIRST THING IN THE MORNIN' I DO BE IN ME ACTUAL HORRORS.

WHEN YE GET BITTEN
BY A MILLION POXY MOSQUITOES

I'VE THE TYPE OF BLOOD THA' MOSQUITOES LOVE TO GET A LIL' SUP OF. IT'S CALLED TYPE O-NLY MASSIVE. NO BUT SWEAR, THOUGH. YE CAN'T TAKE ME POXY ANYWHERE WITHOUT GETTIN' BITTEN A MILLION TIMES BY THE POXES, ESPECIALLY IN THE NIGH' TIME. THERE'S SOME BUG SPRAY THA' YE CAN GET AN' THEY HATE THE TASTE OF IT, AN' IT MEANS THA' YE CAN WALK AROUND BITE-FREE AN' ENJOY YIZZER HOLIDAY.

BLOOD TYPES

THESE ARE SOME OF THE OTHER BLOOD TYPES THA' THE LIL' BASTARDS GO FOR. IF YOU'RE ON THIS LIST THEN YE SHOULD DEFO GET YIZZERSELF THA' ANTI-MOSQUITO SPRAY TO SAVE YE FROM GETTIN' BITTEN TO BITS. THERE'S NO POINT GETTIN' A GOOD TAN ON YIZZER HOLIDAY WHEN YE CAN'T SHOW IT OFF COS YIZZER LEG HAS MORE MOUNTAINS THAN WICKLOW.

TYPE BAG OF CANS
WITH THE LADS

SORRY, THIS IS JUST
A HERSHEY'S KISS, HUN

TYPE MOAN ABOUT
HOW HOT IT IS

TYPE THINKS
THEY'RE GOD'S
BLEEDIN' GIFT

TYPE TANK TOP
WITH HAIRY
ARMPITS

TYPE LEFT THE DOOR
OPEN AN' ALL THE
MOSQUITOES CAME IN

POXES WHO STING YE FOR NO REASON

DO YE MIND? I WAS SUNBATHIN' HERE AN' YE JUST STOOD ON ME FACE, YE TICK

I'LL STING YE AGAIN, YE POX

YE EVER GET STUNG BY A JELLYFISH? THE PURE PAIN OF IT, SWEAR! I WAS PURE SOBBIN' THE FIRST TIME IT HAPPENED TO ME, AN' TANYA WAS THERE LAUGHIN' AT ME. DIDN'T TALK TO HER FOR THREE AN' A HALF DAYS AFTER. THEY SAY THA' IF YE PISS ON YIZZER LEG IT HELPS, BUT I'M TELLIN' YE NOW THA' IT DOES FUCK ALL. SALT WATER IS MEANT TO BE GOOD, AN' IF YE USE VINEGAR AN' BAKIN' SODA AN' MIX IT UP IT TAKES THE STING OUT.

WHEN YE SEE A SHARK

TANYA SAYS TO ME WHEN WE WERE IN KUSADASI LAST YEAR, 'NIKITA, LOOK! A DOLPHIN!' AN' I SAYS TO MESELF, 'WHA' IS SHE ON ABOUT? A POXY DOLPHIN'. SO I LOOK OUT INTO THE WATER AN' IT'S A BLEEDIN' SHARK, AN' I'M LIKE, 'TANYA, SWIM! THERE'S A SHARK!' THE POX WAS SCREAMIN' AN' SWIMMIN' LIKE A MAD YOKE. SHE WAS GRAND IN THE END BUT MORAL OF THE STORY, IF YE THINK YE SEE A DOLPHIN, IT'S MORE THAN LIKELY A SHARK.

TOURIST POXES

IF YE HAVE THESE FOUR THINGS, YOU'RE THE ULTIMATE TOURIST POX AN' MAKIN' YIZZERSELF RIPE FOR A ROBBIN'. WOULD YE WEAR A CAMERA AROUND YOUR NECK WALKIN' AROUND TOWN? PROBABLY NOT, SO WHY WOULD YE DO IT WHEN YOU'RE AWAY? THERE'S NOTHIN' AS BAD AS BEIN' ROBBED ON YIZZER HOLIDAY.

FANNY PACK FULL OF MONEY THA' JUST CLIPS OFF AT THE BACK

FANCY CAMERA AROUND YIZZER NECK FOR ALL TO SEE

SOCKS AN' SANDALS ARE A DEAD GIVEAWAY - THEY'RE ALSO FASHION CONTRACEPTION

HAT TO KEEP YIZZER NECK PROTECTED BUT THAT'S NO USE WHEN YE GET ROBBED, PAL

WHEN GOOGLE MAPS BRINGS YE THE WRONG WAY

GO DOWN THIS DODGY
LANE TO REACH YIZZER
DESTINATION OF DEATH

EVERYONE PUTS THEIR TRUST IN THE GOOGLE MAPS, BUT I TELL
YE SOMETHIN' NOW, THERE'S BEEN A FEW TIMES ME AN' ANTO
HAVE USED IT AN' IT'S BROUGHT US DOWN SOME MAD DODGY
ROADS SAYIN' THA' IT'S A SHORTCUT AN' ALL. YEAH, A SHORTCUT
TO ME POXY COFFIN. IT'S ALL WELL AN' GOOD USIN' THE APP BUT
JUST BE CAREFUL WHERE YOUS ARE WALKIN' COS GOOGLE MAPS
DOESN'T KNOW EVERYTHIN'.

POXES WHO SNORE BESIDE YE

YOU'VE JUST PUT YIZZER PHONE DOWN AN' YOU'RE READY TO GO ASLEEP, AN' THE POX WHO'S SITTIN' BESIDE YE ON THE PLANE IS TAKIN' UP BOTH ARM RESTS AN' SNORIN' LIKE AN' ABSOLUTE BEAST. YOU'RE GONNA BE ON THE PLANE FOR FOUR HOURS SO YE KNOW FULL WELL THA' THIS COULD GO ON FOR THE WHOLE JOURNEY. ME BOLLOX I'D SIT THERE LISTENIN' TO THA'!

WHEN YE CAN'T DEAL

PUT A SMELLY SOCK OVER THE POX'S FACE AN' SEE IF IT WAKES THEM UP.

POKE THEM WITH A STICK. I ALWAYS POKE ANTO WITH A HARRY POTTER WAND.

'ACCIDENTALLY' POUR A GLASS OF WATER OVER THE TICK AN' PRETEND TO BE ASLEEP WHEN THEY WAKE UP.

YOUR LAST AN' ONLY HOPE IS SOME EAR PLUGS. OTHER THAN THA', ALL YE CAN DO IS KEEP POKIN' THE POX.

WHEN YE DRINK TAP WATER ON HOLIDAY

EVERYONE KNOWS THA' THE WATER IN SOME COUNTRIES IS ROTTEN AN' YOU'RE NOT TO DRINK TAP WATER OR HAVE ICE. BUT WHA' HAPPENS WHEN YE HAVE A SNEAKY FANTA AN' VODKA AN' THE POX PUTS ICE IN IT, AN' BY THE TIME YOU'VE REALISED IT THE DRINK IS ALREADY GONE? YOUR STOMACH STARTS MAKIN' NOISES SOON AFTER AN' YE KNOW THIS ISN'T GONNA END WELL, SO WHA' DO YE DO?

WHEN YE HAVE TO GO, YE HAVE TO GO

YE GO TO THE BLEEDIN' JAX IS WHA' YE DO. YEAH, IT MIGH' LOOK
LIKE A CRIME SCENE AFTER YOU'RE DONE, BUT SURE WHO EVEN
KNOWS YE? YOU'RE IN A DIFFERENT COUNTRY AN' YE MORE THAN
LIKELY WON'T SEE THE POXES AGAIN, SO YE MIGH' AS WELL LET IT
COME OUT OF YE AN' JUST STRUT OUT OF THE PLACE LIKE A BOSS,
LIKE NOTHIN' EVEN HAPPENED.

WHEN THERE'S NO AIR CON IN YIZZER ROOM

WHEN THERE'S NO COLD SIDE
TO THE PILLOW. WELCOME TO
HOLIDAY HELL, HUN.

YE KNOW WHEN YE GET TO YIZZER APARTMENT OR WHEREVER AFTER
BEIN' ON THE PLANE FOR HOURS, AN' YE REALISE THA' THERE'S NO
AIR CONDITIONIN' AN' YOU'RE PURE SWEATIN'? THE PLACE IS SO
WARM THA' THERE'S NO COLD SIDE TO THE PILLOW. BEST THING YE
CAN DO IS GET A HOT WATER BOTTLE AN' FILL IT UP WITH COLD
WATER. TELLIN' YE, IT WORKS BRILLIANT AN' YE CAN HAVE YIZZER
COLD SIDE OF THE PILLOW BACK.

BEACH TOWELS SO NO ONE WILL ROB YIZZER SPOT

EVERYONE WANTS TO GO DOWN TO THE POOL FIRST THING IN THE MORNIN' TO GRAB A GOOD SEAT FOR GETTIN' YIZZER TAN ON. SOMETIMES YE DO GET POXES GETTIN' UP AT 12 AN' THEY STRUT DOWN AN' MOVE YIZZER TOWELS. DON'T KNOW WHO THEY THINK THEY BLEEDIN' ARE. I DO ALWAYS GET MESELF A BEACH TOWEL THA' HAS A REAL 'DON'T FUCK WITH ME' FEEL TO IT TO SCARE THE TICKS OFF.

POXES
IN SHOPS

ONE OF THE PLACES YOU'RE ALMOST GUARANTEED TO COME ACROSS A
WILD POX IS IF YE WORK IN RETAIL, BUT ALSO IF YOU'RE JUST DOIN' A
BIT OF SHOPPIN' YIZZERSELF. THIS CHAPTER GOES THROUGH EVERYTHIN'
FROM THINGS FOUND IN CHANGIN' ROOMS AN' SHOPPIN' WITH YIZZER
FELLA TO WHEN SHOPS SAY A SIZE 10 IS A POXY LARGE - ME BOLLOX
IT IS.

SHOP ASSISTANT POX

COULDN'T GIVE A
RAT'S WHA' YOU'RE
LOOKIN' FOR →

TEXTIN' UNDER
THE TABLE
WHILE YOU'RE
TALKIN' TO
THEM

DO YE EVER JUST GO INTO A SHOP IN A GREAT MOOD AN' YOUR WAN
BEHIND THE TILL STARTS GIVIN' YE MOUTH FOR NO OTHER REASON
THAN SHE DOESN'T WANT TO BE IN WORK? I HATE POXES LIKE THA',
AN' THEY'D WANT TO TAKE A LONG HARD LOOK AT THEMSELVES COS
THEY'RE LUCKY THEY EVEN HAVE A POXY JOB IN THIS COUNTRY.

THINGS THEY DO

THE PRICE SAYS THA' IT'S
10 EURDO AN' THEY SAY
IT'S 15, BUT WON'T GIVE
YE THE DISCOUNT EVEN
THOUGH THEY'RE WRONG.

WHEN YE TRY TO BRING
SOMETHIN' BACK WITH A
RECEIPT AN' THEY'RE HAVIN'
NONE OF IT AN' WON'T TAKE
IT BACK.

THEY MAKE A SHOW OF YE
AN' TELL YE THA' THEY
DON'T DO YOUR SIZE.

SAY THA' THEY'VE CHECKED
THE BACK FOR IT BUT YE
KNOW FULL WELL THA' THEY
HAVE IN THEIR BOLLOX.

WHEN A CUSTOMER IS BEIN' A SAP

AT THE OTHER END OF THE SCALE, I'VE HAD SOME CUSTOMERS GOIN' ON A MAD ONE AT ME FOR NO POXY REASON. YE DO BE JUST THINKIN' TO YIZZERSELF, 'WHO EVEN IS THIS YOKE? GET OUT OF ME FACE, YE TICK, IT'S ONLY A PAIR OF FANNY PADS'. BUT YE CAN'T SAY ANYTHIN' COS SOME SAP BACK IN THE EIGHTEEN HUNDREDS MADE UP THE RULE THA' THE POX IS ALWAYS RIGH'.

WHEN YE GO TO PENNEYS TO GET SOCKS

JUST GOIN' IN FOR A QUICK LOOK.
BE ONLY FIVE MINUTES.

EVERYONE I KNOW ALWAYS GOES INTO PENNEYS FOR SOMETHIN' STUPID LIKE ANKLE SOCKS, AN' THEY ALWAYS COME OUT OF THE SHOP WITH 16 BAGS FULL OF CRAP THA' THEY DON'T EVEN NEED BUT WERE TOO CHEAP TO LEAVE THERE. I'M ALWAYS AT IT! YE SHOULD SEE ME DA'S ATTIC — IT'S FULL OF PENNEYS BAGS COS I GET ALL ME PRESENTS FOR THE KIDDIES AN' SAVE THEM THERE FOR DIFFERENT OCCASIONS.

WHEN A POX GETS MAKE-UP ALL OVER THE LAST TOP IN YIZZER SIZE

MAKE-UP ALL
OVER THE NECK

SOMEONE'S BLEEDIN'
COFFEE STAIN

I HATE WHEN YE SEE A MASSIVE TOP AN' IT'S THE ONLY ONE LEFT IN YIZZER SIZE AN' SOME DONKEY IS AFTER GETTIN' MAKE-UP ALL OVER THE POXY THING. NO RESPECT FOR ANYONE ELSE, I TELL YE. NOT BEIN' FUNNY, BUT SOMETIMES THERE'S MORE MAKE-UP ON THE SHIRT THAN THERE IS ON ME BLEEDIN' FACE. SOMETIMES YE CAN GET A SNEAKY DISCOUNT AN' IT'S WELL WORTH IT IF YE KNOW HOW TO TAKE THE STAINS OUT.

WHEN A SHOP SAYS A SIZE 10 IS A LARGE

ARE YE HAVIN' A POXY LAUGH? NO WONDER THE YOUNG WANS TODAY ARE OBSESSED WITH BEIN' SKINNY IF YOU'RE SAYIN' A SIZE 10 IS A LARGE! DON'T KNOW WHAT'S HAPPENIN' TO THE WORLD, BUT ALL THE FASHION POXES WOULD WANT TO COP BLEEDIN' ON IF THEY THINK A SIZE 10 IS LARGE. HUNS, BE HAPPY WITH WHATEVER SIZE YE ARE AN' DON'T LET A SHOP EVER MAKE YE FEEL BAD FOR IT. PACK OF CLOWNS.

WHEN YE WORK IN RETAIL

IF YE WORK IN RETAIL, YOU'LL KNOW THA' THE STRUGGLE OF DAY-TO-DAY THINGS CAN BE DRAININ'. BUT WORKIN' IN FASHION RETAIL BRINGS A WHOLE NEW PACK OF WILD ANIMALS WITH IT. YE DON'T REALISE HOW FILTHY SOME POXES ARE UNTIL YE WORK IN TOWN AN' YE COME ACROSS ALL SORTS OF THINGS IN CHANGIN' ROOMS, LET ME TELL YE. THESE ARE SOME OF THE THINGS I'VE FOUND IN CHANGIN' ROOMS OVER THE YEARS.

THINGS FOUND IN CHANGIN' ROOMS

USED TAMPON

PUT IT IN THE BIN, YE TICK.
I DON'T WANT TO TOUCH IT.

PISS IN A BAG

TESCO

ARE YE HAVIN' A LAUGH, LIKE?
THE JAX IS TWO MINUTES AWAY!

USED JOHNNY

OUT OF ALL THE PLACES,
A PACKED DRESSIN' ROOM.
FILTHY POXES.

SHIT

IF YE WIPE YIZZER ARSE ON THE
CURTAIN, I DON'T CARE WHA'
ANYONE SAYS, YOU'RE AN' ANIMAL.

POXES WHO STROLL INTO SHOPS WHEN THEY'RE CLOSIN'

IT'S THE END OF THE DAY AN' YOU'VE BEEN IN NINE TO SIX. YOU'RE DYIN' TO GO HOME BUT IT'S QUARTER PAST SIX AN' THERE'S SOME SAP STILL WALKIN' AROUND THE SHOP PRETENDIN' THA' THEY HAVE NO IDEA THA' IT'S CLOSED, DESPITE THERE BEIN' NO ONE IN THE JAYSUSIN' SHOP. IF YOU'RE ONE OF THESE POXES, GIVE IT OVER. COME IN DURIN' OPENIN' HOURS COS YOU'RE STOPPIN' ME FROM GETTIN' HOME EARLY.

POXES IN TOY SHOPS

IF ME YOUNG FELLA DOESN'T GET A FIDGET SPINNER, HE SAID HE WON'T SLEEP FOR A WEEK. YE HAVE TO HELP ME!

I USED TO WORK IN SMYTHS AN' YOU'D BE SURPRISED AT THE POXES YE SEE IN THERE. YE WOULD THINK IT WOULD BE THE KIDS THA' ANNOY YE, BUT IT'S THE PARENTS. YE DO ALWAYS GET THEM COMIN' IN AN' SAYIN', 'DID YE SEE WHA' THA' LIL' FELLA WITH THE GLASSES HAD ON THE TOY SHOW?' AN' YE SAY 'NO' AN' THEY'RE SO SURPRISED THA' YE DIDN'T WATCH THE POXY THING. I HAVE A LIFE OUTSIDE ME POXY JOB, YE KNOW.

FACES YIZZER FELLA
MAKES WHEN YOU'RE SHOPPIN'

WHENEVER YE GO SHOPPIN' WITH YIZZER FELLA, NINE TIMES OUT OF TEN HE'S BORED STIFF AN' COULDN'T GIVE A BOLLOX ABOUT WHA' YOU'RE WEARIN' TO THE CHRISTENIN' AT THE WEEKEND. THIS IS A CHART OF ALL THE FACES YIZZER FELLA MAKES AN' WHA' THEY MEAN.

WHEN YE GO INTO A SHOP
WITH THREE FLOORS

WHEN YOU'VE BEEN IN
THE CHANGIN' ROOM
OVER AN HOUR

WHEN YE SAY YE
CAN'T FIND ANYTHIN'
AFTER FIVE HOURS

WHEN IT'S CUTTIN'
INTO MATCH TIME

WHEN HE'S TOLD YE
'THAT'S NICE' FOR
THE FIFTEENTH TIME

WHEN YOU'RE
FINISHED SHOPPIN'

THINGS TO KEEP HIM HAPPY

CAN'T GO WRONG WITH AN
AUL 99 WITH RED SAUCE

BRING HIM TO THE PUB
AFTER FOR THE MATCH

SHAKE YIZZER KEYS EVERY SO
OFTEN TO GIVE THE ILLUSION
THA' YE MIGH' BE LEAVIN' SOON

BRING HIM TO THE LEISUREPLEX
ZOO AFTER SO HE CAN PLAY
IN THE BALL PIT

POXES WHO TRY TO SELL YE EXTENSIONS

PAL, EXTENSIONS WON'T GO IN THIS. DON'T BE LYIN'.

THERE'S NOTHIN' WORSE THAN WHEN YE HAVE SHORT HAIR OR YOU'RE THE IMAGE OF PHIL MITCHELL AN' SOMEONE STARTS TRYIN' TO SELL YE EXTENSIONS. SWEAR, SOME OF THE YOUNG WANS THA' DO BE GETTIN' ASKED IF THEY WANT EXTENSIONS I KNOW FOR A FACT THE THINGS WOULDN'T EVEN STAY IN THEIR HAIR. A GUST OF POXY WIND AN' THEY'D BE GONE.

SPOILED POXES

MA, I WANT AN IPHONE!

YE SEE THE KIDS OF TODAY? SPOILED POXES HALF OF THEM ARE. STRUTTIN' AROUND WITH IPHONES AN' THEY'RE POXY FIVE. WHEN I WAS FIVE, PAL, I HAD A BAG OF MARBLES. I KNOW TIMES ARE CHANGIN' BUT THA' DOESN'T MEAN A FIVE-YEAR-OLD SHOULD HAVE AN IPHONE JUST COS ALL THEIR FRIENDS HAVE ONE. YOU'RE JUST LETTIN' YIZZERSELF INTO A TRAP COS THEY BRING A NEW ONE OUT EVERY POXY YEAR.

WHEN YE HOLD THE
DOOR OPEN FOR SOMEONE AN' THEY DON'T SAY THANKS

EHH!
YOU'RE WELCOME

YE EVER DO YOUR GOOD DEED FOR THE DAY AN' HOLD THE DOOR OPEN FOR PEOPLE COMIN' OUT OF THE SHOPS, AN' YE WOULDN'T EVEN MIND BUT THE DOOR IS HEAVY AN' SOME OF THE POXES DON'T EVEN LOOK AT YE AN' SAY THANKS? LUV, IF I WANTED TO BE A BROWN THOMAS POXY DOORMAN I'D DO IT AN' GET PAID. I THINK IT'S THE HEIGHT OF POXY IGNORANCE TO IGNORE SOMEONE HOLDIN' A DOOR OPEN FOR YE LIKE YOU'RE POXY ROYALTY.

WHA' YE CAN DO

HERE, LUV, YE DROPPED SOMETHIN' VERY IMPORTANT

- CALL THEM AN' TELL THEM THA' THEY DROPPED SOMETHIN'.

- HOLD THE DOOR OPEN FOR THEM AGAIN AN' WATCH THEM WALK IN AN' LOOK FOR WHA' THEY DROPPED.

- WHEN THEY GO TO COME BACK OUT LET THE DOOR GO SO THEY HAVE TO OPEN IT FOR THEMSELVES.

WHEN YOUR ONE ON THE TILL IS HAVIN' A CHA' WITH MARY

SOMETIMES WHEN YOU'RE IN A RUSH TO GET BACK HOME TO WATCH THE SOAPS YE DO HAVE SOMEONE IN THE SHOP TALKIN' TO THEIR FRIEND ON THE OTHER TILL LIKE YOU'RE NOT EVEN STANDIN' THERE. LIKE, I HAVE SOMEWHERE TO POXY BE AN' YOU'RE JUST SITTIN' THERE HAVIN' A FULL-BLOWN CONVO ABOUT HOW THA' FAIR CITY KATY YOUNG WAN'S EYEBROWS LOOK GREAT AFTER BEIN' LOCKED UP FOR A YEAR. WRECKS ME HEAD.

WHEN SHOPS ONLY HAVE CROP TOPS

WHY DO YE
DO THIS TO US?

EVERY TIME I SEE A MASSIVE TOP IN A SHOP I PICK IT UP AN' IT'S
A BLEEDIN' CROP TOP. DON'T GET ME WRONG, THEY LOOK MASSIVE
ON SOME PEOPLE, BUT I COULD NEVER GET AWAY WITH WEARIN' ONE
OR ME DIDDIES WOULD FALL OUT OF THE OTHER END OF THE POXY
THING. HAPPENED TO TANYA ONCE IN SIN AN' NOW WE'RE BARRED.
EVERYONE WAS SCREAMIN'. YE SWEAR THESE YOUNG WANS NEVER
SEEN A BIG DIDDIE IN THEIR WHOLE LIVES.

EXTRA BITS

THIS CHAPTER IS FULL OF EXTRA BITS AN' PIECES LIKE SOAP DRINKIN' GAMES, STUNNIN' HOROSCOPES AN' QUIZZES. THERE'S EVEN A POX STARTER PACK AN' A POX REPELLENT PACK, ALONG WITH ME TOP EVIL POXES THROUGHOUT HISTORY.

DEAR NIKITA
REAL-LIFE PROBLEMS AN' ALL

I FELL IN LOVE WITH A FOUNTAIN

HEY NIKITA,

EVERY SUNDAY I GO UP TO THE FOUNTAIN IN THE OMNI TO SPEND SOME TIME WITH MY MAN, EXCEPT MY MAN IS THE FOUNTAIN. I AM SO IN LOVE. SECURITY HAVE STOPPED FILLING IT UP TO STOP ME FROM SWIMMING IN IT. I DON'T KNOW WHAT TO DO ...

NIKITA: NOT BEIN' FUNNY, HUN, BUT IF YE WANT TO GO SWIMMIN' THERE'S A MASSIVE POOL AROUND THE CORNER IN BALLYMUN. YE CAN'T BE SWIMMIN' IN THE ONE UP IN THE OMNI COS THERE'S KIDDIES AROUND WITH THEIR FAMILIES, AN' THERE YE ARE TALKIN' TO YOUR FELLA WHO'S THE FOUNTAIN. THE POOR KIDDIES WOULDN'T KNOW WHA' WAS GOIN' ON, LUV. I THINK YE NEED TO DOWNLOAD THA' TINDER APP AN' GIVE LUV A GO ONE LAST TIME BEFORE YE SETTLE FOR THE OMNI FOUNTAIN, HUN. COS EVEN THOUGH FOUNTAINS ARE LOVE-LY AN' ALL, THEY CAN'T MOVE SO YE CAN'T BRING THEM HOME. AN' EVEN MORE IMPORTANTLY, THEY HAVE NO POXY MICKEY.

BOSS BITCH

FREE zimmerframe
IN NEXT ISSUE

CRYING FOR PRINGLES ?

HEYA KITA,

I CAN'T STOP CRYIN' EVERY TIME I SEE A CAN OF PRINGLES, HUN. DON'T KNOW WHAT'S WRONG WITH ME.

NIKITA: TENNER BETS YOU'RE PREGGERS, HUN. WHY ELSE WOULD YE BE CRYIN' OVER A CAN OF PRINGLES? GO AN' GET YIZZERSELF A PREGO TEST IN TESCO AN' SEE.

SCHINDLER'S FIST !

HIYA NIKITA,

I WANT TO FIST ME MOTH BUT ME HANDS ARE LIKE THE HULK. WHA' SHOULD I DO?

NIKITA: YE CAN START BY NOT WRITIN' FAKE STORIES INTO ME COLUMN, YE TICK. SWEAR, NOTHIN' BETTER TO DO.

I HAVE FIVE NIPPLES !

HEY NIKITA,

SO, A LOT OF PEOPLE DON'T KNOW, BUT I'VE ACTUALLY GOT FIVE NIPPLES. I HAVE TWO ON THE SOLE OF MY LEFT FOOT AND ONE ON MY BACK. MY BOYFRIEND THINKS THEY'RE CUTE MOLES BUT I HAVEN'T GOT THE HEART TO TELL HIM. I'M TERRIFIED THAT ONE DAY I'LL GET TURNED ON TO THE MAX AN HE'LL SEE THEM. I'M ALSO TERRIFIED THAT IF I GET PREGNANT I'LL HAVE TO PUMP MILK FROM MY FEET. PEOPLE ARE ALREADY WEIRDED OUT BY BREASTFEEDING IN PUBLIC, BUT PUMPING FEET?! WHAT CAN I DO?

NIKITA: AH, VERY SORRY TO HEAR THA', HUN. VERY SORRY INDEED. HAVE YE TRIED GOIN' IN TO GET THEM REMOVED? LIKE, I WOULDN'T SAY IT BE THA' BAD. JUST TELL HIM THE TRUTH. YE NEVER KNOW, HE COULD BE MAD INTO YOUNG WANS WITH FIVE NIPPLES. AT LEAST YE CAN SAY YE REALLY ARE ONE IN A MILLION, HUN.

HOROSCOPES

ARIES

EVERYONE SAYS THA' YOU'RE ALWAYS ON EDGE AN' A BIT AGRO. TAKE TIME TO CHILL OUT SO YE DON'T GET MAD STRESSED OVER POXES BEIN' TICKS. LOOK AFTER NO.1, HUN.

TAURUS

YOU'RE THE LIFE OF THE PARTY AN' THERE'S BIG THINGS COMIN' YIZZER WAY. YE HAVE SOME BIG DECISIONS TO MAKE ABOUT THE FUTURE. KEEP HAVIN' FUN AN' ALWAYS BE YIZZERSELF.

GEMINI

YOU'RE ALWAYS GIVIN' OUT OVER LIL' THINGS. LOOK AT THE BIGGER PICTURE AN' START MAKIN' YIZZER OWN PLANS NOW. STOP RELYIN' ON POXES TO MAKE PLANS WITH YE, HUN.

CANCER

YE HAVEN'T GOT A BAD BONE IN YIZZER BODY AN' YOU'RE ALWAYS THERE TO HELP OTHERS. IT'S TIME YE TREAT YIZZERSELF AN' GO ON AN ADVENTURE SOMEWHERE.

LEO

YOU'RE THE IMAGE OF A BOILED EGG BUT YE NEVER LET THA' STOP YE. I CAN SEE YE GETTIN' A LOVELY FELLA IN THE FUTURE. KEEP YIZZER EYES PEELED FOR HIM, HUN.

VIRGO

YOU'RE THE PURE DEFINITION OF A POX. YOU'RE ALWAYS COMPLAININ', ALWAYS MOANIN'. WOULD YE EVER GIVE IT OVER AN' GO OUT AN' ENJOY YIZZERSELF? LIFE'S TOO SHORT TO BE A SAP.

LIBRA

2018 IS YOUR YEAR, LUV. IT'S GONNA BE FULL OF HOPE, MONEY AN' HONDA CIVICS. YOU'VE HAD A SHIT YEAR BUT YIZZER LUCK IS ABOUT TO CHANGE FOR THE BETTER.

SCORPIO

YE LOOK LIKE A RUBBER ARMBAND BY DAY BUT A SEXY SEAGULL BY NIGH'. OWN IT, HUN. YOU'RE THE BEST LOOKIN' PERSON IN THE POXY ROOM. YE COULD BE THE NEXT KIMMY K.

SAGITTARIUS

DON'T LOOK BACK IN ANGER. MOVE ON. THERE'S PLENTY OF DECENT FELLAS OUT THERE AN' YE JUST HAVEN'T FOUND HIM YET. STOP TRYIN' SO HARD AN' IT WILL HAPPEN WHEN YE LEAST EXPECT IT.

CAPRICORN

YE SMELL LIKE A NEW CAR AN' YE LOOK LIKE ONE TOO. YE HAVE IT ALL GOIN' FOR YE. YE JUST NEED TO STOP STRESSIN' AN' THINGS WILL FIGURE THEMSELVES OUT. LOOK TO THE FUTURE.

AQUARIUS

YE BITCH BEHIND ALL YIZZER HUNS' BACKS AN THEN YOU'RE ALL NICE TO THEIR FACES? DO YOURSELF A FAVOUR AN' GO SWIVEL ON THE NIPPLE OF ME LEFT DIDDIE, YE POX.

PISCES

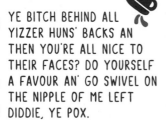

EVERYONE SAYS YE LOOK LIKE A CAMEL BUT I CAN'T SEE IT. YE KNOW WHA' THEY SAY, HUN: HATERS GONNA HATE. WHEN YE HAVE HATERS THA' MEANS YOU'VE MADE IT. AN' YOU'VE A LOAD OF 'EM, HUN.

IN THE FADED LIGHT YE TOUCH ME NAGGIN

KISS ME
FLAPS
AN' GO SWIVEL
ON THE
NIPPLE
OF ME LEFT
DIDDIE

I TOOK A PILL IN IBIZA. NO, PAL, YE HAD A FEW TIC TACS ON YOUR HOLLIERS IN YOUR MOBILE HOME IN WEXFORD.

ehhh
Sorry
'Bout ye

★ SOAP ★ DRINKIN' GAME

WHA'?

EMMERDALE

THERE'S USUALLY A DOUBLE EMMERDALE ON THURSDAY, AN' THEY SAY THURSDAY IS THE NEW FRIDAY SO WHA' ELSE WOULD YE BE DOIN' OTHER THAN PRE-DRINKIN' AN' CATCHIN' UP ON THE SOAPS AS YE GO ALONG? PLUS YE GET TO STARE AT ROSS FOR A FULL HOUR. HE'S MASSIVE. DO ALWAYS ASK ANTO TO GET HIS HAIR CUT LIKE HIM.

THE RULES

- TAKE A SUP WHEN ZAK SAYS 'FLIPPIN' HECK'.
- TAKE TWO SUPS WHEN LACHLAN IS BEIN' A CREEP.
- TAKE FOUR SUPS WHENEVER DAN'S BEIN' A LIL' BITCH.
- DANCE LIKE A SAP WHEN MARLON IS WEARIN' HIS CHEF GEAR.
- ANOTHER SUP IF YE SEE VIC IN HER CHEF GEAR TOO.
- TAKE THREE SUPS EVERY TIME KERRY SAYS 'MAN'.
- DOWN YIZZER DRINK IF SOMEONE ORDERS A COFFEE TO GO IN THE CAFÉ.
- TAKE A SUP EVERY TIME ERIC IS GOIN' ON A MAD ONE.
- DOWN YIZZER DRINK EVERY TIME YE SEE DEBBIE FROWN.
- DOWN YIZZER DRINK EVERY TIME CHARITY IS UP TO NO GOOD.
- TAKE A SUP EVERY TIME ROSS IS UP TO SOMETHIN'.
- TAKE A SUP WHEN MEGAN IS BEIN' A POX TO JAI.

DRAW A POX

ALL YE NEED FOR THIS GAME IS SOME PENS AN' PIECES OF PAPER AN' A
MAXIMUM OF SIX PLAYERS. WE PLAY THIS ALL THE TIME IF WE'RE HAVIN'
A SESSION IN TANYA'S MA'S GAFF. DO BE ON THE FLOOR ROLLIN' AROUND
LAUGHIN' SOMETIMES. HERE'S THE RULES FOR THE GAME.

THE RULES

- EACH POX HAS A GO AT BEIN' THE TIMER AN' BEIN' THE
  GOOD DRAWER.
- THE TIMER WILL WHISPER A FAMOUS POX TO THE DRAWER AND START
  THE TIMER.
- IF YE CAN GUESS WHO IT IS BY THE DRAWIN', YE CAN SHOUT OUT THE
  ANSWER.
- EACH PERSON GETS TO ASK A QUESTION ABOUT THE FAMOUS POX.
- FOR EVERY 15 SECONDS THA' PASS, YE HAVE TO TAKE A SUP OF YIZZER
  DRINK.
- THESE CAN BE POXES FROM THE TV, MOVIES, POLITICIANS, ANYONE!
  JUST ONCE THEY'RE HUMAN. THAT'S ALL YE NEED TO KNOW TO PLAY.

WHEN YOUR MA'S A POX

CAN SEE RIGH' THROUGH YE LIKE A SHIT PAIR OF LEGGINS

LOOKS OUT THE WINDOW WHEN THERE'S A FIGH' ON YIZZER ROAD BUT IN THE DARK SO NO ONE CAN SEE HER

HAS A HEART OF DUTCH GOLD

ENTERS EVERY COMPETITION EVER POSTED IN THE HISTORY OF FACEBOOK AN' STILL HASN'T WON A POXY THING

LOVES AN AUL LIFE QUOTE ON THE FACEBOOK AN' IS ALWAYS ON THE BUY AN' SELL PAGES

SAYS SHE DOESN'T NEED ANY HELP BUT THEN GIVES OUT TO YE FOR NOT HELPIN' HER

OWNS A HIMALAYAN SALT LAMP

LEGS FOR BOOTIN' YE UP THE STAIRS WHEN YE GET CAUGHT DRINKIN'

WHAT'S YOUR POX NAME?

MONTH YE WERE BORN		FIRST LETTER OF YIZZER NAME	
JAN	LOVELY	A CURLY NIPPLES	N EGG HATCHER
FEB	STUNNIN'	B DIDDIE FIDDLER	O POGO STICK MICKEY
MAR	MASSIVE	C MICKEY FEELER	P SNAKE STRADDLER
APR	SAGGY	D PICKLE SUCKER	Q HOOP MUNCHER
MAY	MC	E FLAP FOLDER	R TESCO WINE SICK
JUN	DR	F CURTAIN STROKER	S CURRY TAMPON FOOL
JUL	MISS	G DAMP YOKE	T CODDLE MICKEY
AUG	SIR	H ARSE CLENCHER	U RAISIN BALLS
SEP	MADAME	I HOOP HANDLER	V SUPERQUINN SAUSAGE
OCT	MR	J BACK STROKER	W MICKEY FLASHER
NOV	MRS	K BALL HUGGER	X POX WHISPERER
DEC	PROFESSOR	L GARDA GROPER	Y FINGER FIDDLER
		M BEAN MUNCHER	Z FLAP SLAPPER

THINGS POXES SAY

WHERE CAN I GET A FIDGET SPINNER FOR THE YOUNG FELLA?

LIKE, AVOCADO TOAST IS BETTER THAN ACTUAL TOAST.

I DON'T KNOW IF I TOLD YOU BUT I ACTUALLY GO TO TRINITY.

DO YE HAVE A SMOKE? NO? WELL CAN I HAVE AN END OFF OF YE THEN?

TO SLIMMING WORLD GROUP: HOW MANY SYNS IS IN A GRAPE? TIA!

MY DAD OWNS LIKE FIVE BOATS AND ONE OF THEM HAS THREE TOILETS.

POX BADGES

EVIL POXES
THROUGHOUT HISTORY

HERE'S ME LIST OF EVIL POXES THROUGHOUT HISTORY.
THEY SAY THERE'S MORE THAN WHA' MEETS THE EYE AN'
TO NEVER JUDGE A BOOK BY ITS COVER, BUT I WOULDN'T
GET ON THESE POXES' BAD SIDES. I'LL TELL YE THA' MUCH.

MARGARET
THATCHER

URSULA FROM
THE LITTLE MERMAID

THA' HITLER POX

SCAR FROM
THE LION KING

DR EVIL FROM
AUSTIN POWERS

DONALD TRUMP

CHARLES
MANSON

PLANKTON
FROM SPONGEBOB

IT THE CLOWN
- STEPHEN KING

KIM JONG-UN

MR BURNS
FROM THE
SIMPSONS

STEWIE FROM
FAMILY GUY

JOSEPH STALIN

JOAN BURTON

OSAMA BIN LADEN

THE POX STARTER PACK

MAKE SURE YOU'RE WEARIN'
THE LATEST TRENDS AN'
DRESSED EXACTLY THE
SAME AS YIZZER MATES.

HOW TO MAKE
A SHIT LOAD
OF NOISE
DOWN THE
BACK OF THE
BUS

MAKE SURE THA' IF YE GET ON
A BUS YE HAVE TO WRECK
EVERYONE'S HEADS. SHOUT,
SCREAM, PLAY SHIT MUSIC —
THE CHOICES ARE ENDLESS.

DZOPE DIAMONDZ

WEAR BEADS ON YIZZER HEAD
EVEN IF YOU'RE NOT GOIN' TO
A FESTIVAL.

BEYONCÉ DUNNE
DON'T BELIEVE IN
STAR SIGNS
SWEAR I'M OVER 18

GET YIZZERSELF A DECENT ID
SO YE CAN GET INTO THE CLUBS
AN' WRECK EVERYONE'S HEADS IN
THERE TOO.

POX REPELLENT PACK

GIVE THEM THE EYES I SHOWED
YE HOW TO DO ON P.35.

KEEP A CUCUMBER AT THE READY
TO BEAT THE POXES OFF.

WEAR ONE OF THEM HARRY POTTER
INVISIBLE CAPES SO THE POXES
CAN'T SEE YE.

USE A BOTTLE OF LYNX AFRICA TO
SPRAY THEM AWAY IN THE OTHER
DIRECTION.

ACKNOWLEDGEMENTS

I'D LIKE TO THANK ALL THE POXES IN ME LIFE THA' MADE THIS BOOK HAPPEN IN THE FIRST PLACE, COS IF IT WEREN'T FOR YOU SAPS I WOULDN'T HAVE A BOOK AT ALL, SO THANKS.

I'D LIKE TO THANK ME NANNY, MARGARET, FIRST OF ALL FOR LETTIN' ME DO THE BOOK AT THE END OF HER KITCHEN TABLE EVERY DAY AN' HAVIN' THE PATIENCE OF A PURE SAINT WHEN I WAS STRESSED TO BITS.

TO ME DA AN' ME SISTER, DERMOT AND ORLA, FOR SUPPORTIN' ME IN EVERYTHIN' I'VE DONE SO FAR IN ME ACTUAL LIFE, ESPECIALLY WHEN I STARTED NEW ADVENTURES, LIKE DOIN' THE COMEDY AN' ALL.

TO ALL ME FANS, WHETHER YOUS FOLLOW ME ON FACEBOOK, SNAPCHAT, TWITTER OR WHEREVER – DOESN'T MATTER! THIS WOULDN'T BE HAPPENIN' WITHOUT YOUS SO THANKS TO EACH AN' EVERY ONE OF YE FOR SUPPORTIN' ME AN' BUYIN' ME BOOK. YOUS REALLY ARE THE BEST.

TO ALL ME HUNS IN GILL BOOKS FOR PUTTIN' UP WITH ME, CATHERINE GOUGH, TERESA DALY, ELLEN MONNELLY, JEN PATTON AN' SARAH LIDDY, AN' TO ME AGENT, FAITH O'GRADY, FOR BEIN' BANG ON.

TO BASICALLY EVERYONE I KNOW WHO HELPED MAKE THIS HAPPEN AN' SUPPORTED ME ALONG THE WAY.